Park Synagogue

JULY 1996

Presented By:

In Memory Of:

Journeys & Arrivals

By Lev Raphael

Journeys & Arrivals (essays)
Let's Get Criminal (mystery)
Winter Eyes (novel)
Edith Wharton's Prisoners of Shame (criticism)
Dancing on Tisha B'Av (stories)

Coauthored by Lev Raphael

Coming Out of Shame (with Gershen Kaufman)
Dynamics of Power (with Gershen Kaufman)
Stick Up for Yourself! (with Gershen Kaufman)
Teacher's Guide to Stick Up for Yourself (with Gerri Johnson
and Gershen Kaufman)

Journeys & Arrivals

On Being Gay and Jewish

---

by Lev Raphael

Faber and Faber
Boston · London

Library of Congress Cataloging-in-Publication Data
Raphael, Lev.
    Journeys & arrivals : on being gay and Jewish / Lev Raphael.
        p.   cm.
    ISBN 0-571-19882-1 (cloth)
    1. Raphael, Lev.   2. Gay Men—United States—Biography.   3. Jewish
gays—United States—Biography.   4. Children of Holocaust survivors—United
States.   5. Jewish gays—Israel.   6. Gays—Identity.   7. Jews—Identity.
I. Title.
HQ75.8.R36A3   1996
305.38′9664′092—dc20
[B]   95-39070
                                                                                              CIP

Jacket design by David Shultz
Jacket photograph by Richard Lee / *Detroit Free Press*
Printed in the United States of America

For, while the tale of how we suffer, and how we are delighted, and how we may triumph is never new, it must always be heard. There isn't any other tale to tell, it's the only light we've got in all this darkness.

"Sonny's Blues"
JAMES BALDWIN

Acknowledgments

"To Be a Jew" appeared in different form in *Wrestling with the Angel: Faith and Religion in the Lives of Gay Men,* ed. Brian Bouldrey (New York: Riverhead, 1995).

"Okemos, Michigan" originally appeared in different form in *Hometowns: Gay Men Write about Where They Belong,* ed. John Preston (New York: Dutton, 1991). It has also been published in *Living in the USA,* ed. Kathleen Cain (Boston: Allyn & Bacon, 1994).

"Letter from Israel, I" appeared in different form as "Parties, Parks and Politics" in *Christopher Street,* issue 205.

"Losing My Mother: Scenes from a Memoir" appeared in different form in *International Quarterly,* October 1995, vol. II, no. 3.

"Writing Something Real" is a shortened version of "On a Narrow Bridge: A Jewish Writer's Journey," *Reconstructionist,* Spring 1992.

"Letter from Israel, II" appeared in different form as "Letter from Israel" in *Lambda Book Report,* November/December, 1994, vol. 4, no. 7.

"Why Are They Bashing *Dancer from the Dance?*" appeared in *Lambda Book Report,* January/February, 1995, vol. 4, no. 8.

"Selling Was Never My Line" appeared in different form in *The Writing Self,* Winter 1995, vol. 4, no. 1, as "Have Book Out, Will

Travel" in the *Harvard Gay and Lesbian Review,* Summer 1994, and "The Road Warrior" in *Frontiers,* June 4, 1993.

"Domestic and Space Invaders" appeared in different form as "Surviving Close Encounters in the Bronx," *Forward,* June 17, 1994, and "Family Secrets," *Jerusalem Report,* January 12, 1995.

"Judaism's Moral Strength" is drawn from "Abuse of Homosexuals, Jews Has Been Similar," *Lansing State Journal,* January 1, 1993 and "Put Out the Fire," *Detroit Jewish News,* January 22, 1993.

"Dangerous Men" appeared in different form in *Frontiers,* October 8, 1992.

"Empty Memory?" appeared in slightly different form in the *Harvard Gay and Lesbian Review,* Summer 1995.

Contents

Introduction		xiii
1.	*To Be a Jew*	I
2.	*Okemos, Michigan*	33
3.	*Letter from Israel, I*	47
4.	*Losing My Mother: Scenes from a Memoir*	61
5.	*Writing Something Real*	79
6.	*Letter from Israel, II*	89
7.	*Why Are They Bashing* Dancer from the Dance?	97
8.	*Selling Was Never My Line*	107
9.	*Scars*	113
10.	*Domestic and Space Invaders*	121
11.	*Judaism's Moral Strength*	131
12.	*Dangerous Men*	139
13.	*Empty Memory? Gays in Holocaust Literature*	147

Introduction

Introduction

I received the offer to publish this book the same day that a car bomb caused massive devastation in Oklahoma City. While I bounced back and forth all day between elation and dismay, the juxtaposition did not strike me as unusual. For as long as I can remember, I have lived with the imagination of disaster, with the sense that tragedy can strike at any moment, and probably will. Though the bomb didn't physically injure me, it sent the clear and terrifying message that the international scenes of carnage I was used to seeing on television could strike much closer to home. This dread was perfectly described by the Polish-Jewish writer Antoni Slominski: "Behind the stage of our life, concealed in the wings, great factories of suffering are at work that will visit us one day."

From an early age I knew terror had not just stalked my family, but savaged it. My mother's family in Vilno, Poland, had been attending a funeral when Nazi bombs started falling around them in 1941. That was just the beginning in a cycle of terror, ghettoization, forced labor, concentration camps, and death.

Perhaps it was to fight this kind of knowledge that I retreated into books as soon as I could read on my own, barricading myself behind a weekly stack of library loans, reading with dogged intensity to find a way out, or at least a refuge.

I wanted to write books myself from as far back as fourth grade. Lacking talent for any of the visual arts, I found writing the most satisfying and accessible way to express myself. But though I imagined myself an author, and enjoyed all kinds of writing, fiction was always at the center of my vision. It was as a fiction writer that I made my debut in *Redbook* in 1978, and began publishing steadily from 1983 on.

Though I'd published a short coauthored autobiographical piece in the early eighties in the *Baltimore Jewish Times* that has been incorporated into "To Be a Jew," it wasn't until the late John Preston solicited a contribution for his 1991 anthology, *Hometowns: Gay Men Write about Where They Belong* that I turned to writing creative nonfiction. "Okemos, Michigan" was one of the most difficult pieces I ever wrote. Trying to describe buying our house, I kept tormenting myself and my partner Gersh with questions: Is that how it happened? Is this accurate?

I didn't realize then the truth of an observation in Peter Ackroyd's dazzling novel *Chatterton:* "Everything which is written down immediately becomes a kind of fiction." Or, as Janet Malcolm puts it even more trenchantly in *The Silent Woman:* "In a work of nonfiction we almost never know the truth of what happened. The ideal of unmediated reporting is regularly achieved only in fiction, where the writer faithfully reports what is going on in his imagination."

If I'd been asked to write a *story* about two gay Jewish men living in a mid-Michigan suburb, that would have been easy. *Transforming* the material of my own life was something I was used to; recording and shaping it was not. That difficulty was especially ironic since I'm constantly being asked at readings, "How autobiographical is your fiction?"

Frustrated with what I thought was the main demand of an essay about myself—scrupulous accuracy—I dropped "Okemos" mid-way, and it was only the pressure of a deadline that forced me to finish it. I wasn't sure I even liked the piece when I was done.

But the response to that essay from readers was so consistently positive and encouraging that I felt a door had opened for me. I realized that writing an essay about finding and creating a home touched on the central questions of my life, questions implied by the lesbian Jewish poet Melanie Kaye/Kantrowitz in her poem "Notes of an Immigrant Daughter: Atlanta":

> i can't go back
> where i came from was
> burned off the map
>
> i'm a jew
> anywhere is someone else's land

How could I feel comfortable and safe in the world, given what had happened to my parents in the Holocaust? How could I, who felt so separated from other Jews by my upbringing, my parents' past, and my own homosexuality, come to identify with my own people? How could I incorporate my gay identity into my Jewishness? Because I found my first home in books, could reading and writing supply me with the answers to those questions?

This collection weaves together all those questions, and no doubt raises many more. As the Jewish joke my parents were so fond of goes: "Why does a Jew always answer a question with a question? Well, why *shouldn't* a Jew answer a question with a question?"

The essays in this book were published between 1990 and 1995. Wherever they appeared, almost all of them grew in some way out of two extensive book tours for my collection *Dancing on Tisha B'Av* and my novel *Winter Eyes*. I read all across the country at widely different venues like Jewish book fairs, colleges, synagogues, Gay Pride fests, and writers' conferences.

In city after city I was bombarded with very personal questions about my struggles to come out as a Jew and how that process set the stage for coming out as a gay man. These questions were as interesting to me as technical questions about the craft of writing, or spiritual questions about Judaism and homosexuality. Perhaps because my mother and her father were teachers, and I myself had taught at the college level for over a decade, I found myself very comfortable in this new role that went beyond that of the typical writer on tour.

The humorous side of touring never escaped me, however, which is why I felt compelled to write "Selling Was Never My Line."

Describing my coming out at many of these readings, I often told the anecdote involving my college writing teacher that appears in "Writing Something Real," which is drawn from an autobiographical essay I published in the Jewish magazine *Reconstructionist*.

Some of the essays here were occasional pieces, like "Dangerous Men," which I wrote for *Frontiers* in response to the hate-filled speeches at the 1992 Republican Party Convention. Others, like "Judaism's Moral Strength," are drawn from guest editorials I published in the *Lansing State Journal* or the *Detroit Jewish News*.

"Domestic and Space Invaders" is the fruit of my delighted embrace of book reviewing. For years I had resisted doing reviews, thinking it was a form I wouldn't flourish in. But reviewing regularly for the *Detroit Free Press* as well as for the *Jerusalem Report* and other publications has unexpectedly nourished me as a writer.

It's *as* a writer that I penned "Why Are They Bashing *Dancer from the Dance*?" in 1994. Andrew Holleran's "version" of *The Great Gatsby* had come under attack by some prominent gay writers, and I felt pressed to examine why. *Dancer from the Dance* has influenced me more than any other gay novel; the title of my story collection is a reflection of that debt.

The two "Letters from Israel" were written several years apart. The first, framed by the memories of my first trip there in 1978, was an exploration of what gay life was like in the 1980s and early 1990s. The second was a response to a shocking antigay incident I witnessed with my partner Gersh at Israel's Yad Vashem, the Holocaust Memorial Museum in Jerusalem on my second visit there in 1993.

"Empty Memory?" started as a review of books about gays in the Holocaust for the *Harvard Gay and Lesbian Review*. It grew into something much more extensive because I quickly realized that the topic was too big to cover briefly. I also thought it was a good place to explore common misunderstandings about the Holocaust among gays and lesbians, as well as present information about gay suffering under the Nazis to straight Jewish readers. This essay is representative of the cultural work I've been doing ever since my collection came out in 1990: building bridges between various communities, being out as a gay man among Jews, and as a Jew among gays and lesbians.

Just as my fiction had often been sparked by a dialogue with other writers, the newest pieces, "To Be a Jew," "Scars," and "Losing My Mother," grew in response to a series of remarkable and inspiring memoirs that pushed me to explore my own past more deeply. It was impossible for me to read these vivid and original books and not feel the urge to reply: Alice Kaplan's *French Lessons*; Erica Jong's *The Devil at Large* and *Fear of Fifty*; Donald Hall's *Life Work*; Max Lerner's *Wrestling with the Angel*; James Merrill's *A Different Person*; Marianna De Marco Torgovnick's *Crossing Ocean Parkway*; Anatole Broyard's *Kafka Was the Rage*; and Paul Monette's *Becoming a Man*.

But a different, more intimate chorus of voices has also encouraged and stimulated me in many ways to write the essays in this book. My friend Mike Steinberg, a superb essayist, pushed me to put this collection together and send it out. Terri Jewell, Sarita Overton, and Jim Heavenrich gave me much-needed advice and support through some very dark times. Kris Lauer, my college creative writing teacher who appears in several of these essays, has championed my writing since 1972. Everyone should have a best friend like that, especially when the clouds roll in. "Writing Something Real" is a tribute to over two decades of her dedication and friendship.

I'm often asked at readings who my favorite writers are. One of my earliest influences was James Baldwin, whom I first encountered as the author of *Another Country* in my mid-teens, and as an even more dazzling essayist in college. David Leeming's fine biography of Baldwin finds his four major themes present in *Notes of a Native Son*: "the search for identity . . . the acceptance of one's inheritance as one claims one's birthright, the loneliness of the artist's quest, the urgent necessity of love."

Reading that list, I saw in a new way why Baldwin's work had fascinated and inspired me for so long. My fiction and now my essays show parallel concerns: searching for Jewish and gay identity, struggling against and then embracing the inheritance of the Holocaust, examining the hazards of the writer's life.

As for the "necessity of love," that I've found with Gersh Kaufman, my partner of ten years, and our happiness has "been stamped onto every page of my adult life . . . as a watermark," as Edmund White puts it in his wonderful story "Watermark."

This book is dedicated to Gersh, who has earned it many times over.

To Be a Jew

1

To Be a Jew

I was relieved in my late teens when our Washington Heights synagogue, victim of a "changing neighborhood," became some sort of church. I'd only been inside once, for a campaign speech of John Lindsay's, but my father's small dry cleaning store was on the same block, and when I worked there on Saturday mornings while the synagogue was still open, I felt uncomfortable and ashamed. I wished we were closed. Even though we weren't remotely observant, it didn't seem right.

My father, whose childhood and adolescence resembled the devout Eastern European life Elie Wiesel has described in many of his books, had abandoned his religious belief during the war—maybe in Bergen-Belsen, where his father died three days before the Liberation, or earlier, as a slave laborer for the Hungarian Army. Asking him to close the store on *shabbos* would have been foolish.

As I watched from behind the scarred linoleum-covered counter, watched the men and boys in suits, the women lovely and correct, the girls trying to be, I felt alien. I had no idea what they did inside the high-fronted, vaguely Moorish-looking building, only that they did it without me. I had not been bar mitzvahed, and neither had my brother. I suppose I didn't believe it mattered.

3

Although Yiddish newspapers and books filled our home, and my parents' only close friends were other ghetto and concentration camp survivors, I did not identify with them. I did not want to be a Jew.

I wanted to escape.

My earliest intense awareness of myself as a Jew had come in first grade, when an older child told me that "Germans threw Jewish babies in the air and caught them on bayonets." She acted it out while she spoke. This may have been around the time of the Eichmann trial. So, like the lesbian Jewish poet Irena Klefpisz (also a child of Holocaust survivors), "my first conscious feeling about being Jewish was that it was dangerous, something to be hidden."

I can't recall now if I mentioned the incident at home, but I know that afterward, I began to learn at least partial answers to questions that must have been troubling me: Why didn't I have grandparents? Why did my father have terrible nightmares? Where was our family?

As with many families of Holocaust survivors, in my home there was a vast and deafening silence about the Holocaust. Details emerged piecemeal, unexpectedly, painfully. Amid the silence, I was always stepping on mines. Like the time when I was eight or nine, making a hand puppet from an old white sock I'd given a crayoned face. He'd be a superhero because I'd tied a handkerchief around his "neck" to make the cape. But he needed an emblem, which I drew with gold glitter glue: a bolt of lightning. It looked so good I drew a second one and showed it to my mother, expecting praise and smiles.

"That's like the S.S. insignia." She turned away and I felt crushed.

My mother told me only fragments of her ordeals, and my father said next to nothing. I don't think I ever completely understood a very simple truth: People had wanted to *kill* my mother, *kill* my father—and hadn't quite succeeded.

Until I was well into my twenties, I had no Jewish pride at all; I was *ashamed* of being Jewish. I was mortified by my parents' accents when they spoke English (though they spoke a dozen languages between them) and by their use of Yiddish in public because it seemed to stamp us as alien, different, inferior. When I was young I even imagined having a non-Jewish name. Like Tom Danbury, a name I had heard in an Abbott and Costello movie. Think of it: Tom Sawyer crossed with the name of a New England town—what could be more American?

When friends or acquaintances in junior high or high school made anti-Semitic jokes or remarks, I never challenged them. A fierce admirer of Martin Luther King from fourth grade on, I didn't have the courage to speak up for my own people in my own voice. I rarely identified with Jewish causes, except for a visceral support of Israel, and felt a terrible embarrassment when I read something disgraceful about a Jew in the newspapers.

My Jewishness in part consisted of a sensitivity to any threat to American Jews. I had more than a vague idea of the Jewish past, but Torah, prayer, and religious observance of the holidays were all another world, one I didn't even know enough about to truly ignore. It didn't exist. I had no close Jewish friends even though my neighborhood was heavily Jewish, and so were my schools. When I read about Jewish history, I felt both attracted and repelled.

My parents themselves were deeply ambivalent about being Jewish. When I asked them why they'd come to America rather than Israel after World War II, my mother was sharp: "Live with all those Jews? I had enough of them in the ghetto and the camps!" And when I was in first grade and a fire broke out one Friday night in the apartment of Orthodox neighbors, my parents both seemed to blame our neighbors' *shabbat* candles, nodding as if to say, "See, that's what happens . . ."

They didn't know that the neighbor's son and I had once traded views of our nascent penises. One afternoon in my bedroom, we agreed to the exchange, and laughing with nervousness, I stripped completely. I waited for him to do the same, but he only pulled his pants and shorts away from his waist and let me look briefly down. I felt humiliated. With my girl friend Vicky, our genital displays and exploration were completely mutual, which might explain why I felt so cheated and ashamed.

There were other sources for my mother's rage, and other reasons for coming to America. Simply put, "In Brussels, we couldn't stand being so close."

I knew she meant so close to *Germany*. And I knew they missed Belgium. It was obvious in their joyful recollections of the bakery in the first floor of their building whose early morning breads wafted them awake; the squeaky tram line on their street; the delicious fresh vegetables they couldn't seem to find in New York; the elegant and beautiful neighbor who told them *"Je fais les boulevards,"* which they didn't understand meant she was a streetwalker; the oddities and humor of living in a bicultural and bilingual country. Their five years there after the war were to me like some colorful but cloudy ideal to strive after.

My parents had a small battered briefcase filled with tiny black and white photos of monuments, streets, parks, zoo animals—all Belgian. It never occurred to me to ask why they hadn't been neatly hinged into a set of albums. There was to my young imagination something mysterious in the disordered, rustling bulk that shifted when I picked up the peeling butterscotch case with rusty locks and set it onto the floor. Something alive.

Maybe fixing each photograph into a permanent position would have stifled that life for them, crushed the memories. Perhaps what they wanted was the opposite: randomness as a snapshot of a strutting peacock at the zoo slid across a snapshot of a windy beach, scalloped edges catching, bringing the photos into surprising conjunction.

They had very little money in Belgium, moved into an apartment so filthy the black wooden mantel turned out to be white marble after repeated washing. She said they couldn't afford to have children and aborted their first child. Was Belgium truly home? Perhaps it was simply being alive and living in relative comfort after living in hell for so long that had made Brussels wonderful.

"America wasn't our first choice," I heard more than once. My parents had wanted to go to Australia, where friends had emigrated, and made it rich. Australia, of course, was the opposite of Belgium—it was as far away from Germany as you could get.

But America claimed them because of empty promises.

Betrayal was my family's narrative. The great betrayal by the world that had murdered their families, destroyed their homes, their culture, and ripped them out of life. That was central in our family, like the atrium of an ancient Roman home, a place where all can meet and stare above at mystery.

But there were other more intimate betrayals connected to family, and to other Jews.

In Brussels, my mother worked as a teacher in a school that did what we now call "reprogramming." Her students were Jewish children who had been hidden by priests and nuns during the war, and though none of them had been baptized, their minds had been poisoned against Jews and Jewishness. My mother taught Yiddish literature and drama, and at one of the children's performances, New York teachers of Yiddish raved about her work and urged her to come there, promising a job.

Her uncle in New York likewise promised her a new life, and his continued blandishments lured her away.

What did she find in New York? The wonderful apartment her uncle promised her was run down and at the southern shabby end of Washington Heights, more than thirty blocks away from where he lived. My fifth grade teacher said where I lived was Harlem; that street is certainly Harlem now.

Her uncle wouldn't help my mother go back to school

("What'd'ya need college for?"), even though she had done her first
year at the university in Kaunus, Lithuania. And his wife made a
remark that was often repeated to me as proof that she was a miser-
able human being: "You think you had it bad in the war? Here, we
had *rationing*. I had to stand in line for sugar!"

This anecdote would be followed by my parents' withering
Yiddish assessment: "*Azah shtick baheymah!*" (What a horrible
creature).

And the job my mother had been promised didn't exist. The
Jewish educators so impressed by her work in Brussels didn't care
that she was in New York in 1950, and had nothing to offer her but
excuses. Some of these people, fleeing Warsaw in 1939, had wound
up sheltering with her family in Vilno. "They slept on our floor!"

Apparently they had forgotten the favor.

So. American Jews in general didn't help my parents, didn't care
about their uprooted lives, and the Jews who should have been
most concerned—family—didn't seem to care either.

These were the main charges in the indictment my mother had
handed down before I was born.

But despite my parents' contempt for the American-born teachers there, my parents made me go to a Workmen's Circle Sunday
school into my early teens, where I was exposed to Yiddish-language
lessons in Jewish history and literature. I was happy whenever I fell
ill or overslept and didn't have to go to that school. Almost nothing
made an impression on me there, except for one older boy—dark,
sexy, slim—whom I sometimes annoyed because that was the only
way to make him interested in me.

What I remember best of all about my Workmen's Circle classes
happened one day in our excruciatingly dull Torah class, where the
ratio of Hebrew to Yiddish on the page intrigued me. The thick
square of Hebrew words, surrounded by the long Yiddish translation, seemed so dark and dense, impenetrable. We were studying
Koheleth (*Ecclesiastes*), which is still vivid to me because of the "van-

ity of vanities" refrain—"*nishtikeit*" in Yiddish. It seemed powerful to consider this cynicism and despair in three languages.

I was culturally Jewish, or more accurately, the *son* of parents who were culturally Jewish. So I could feel superior, with my father, to the Reform rabbi of the synagogue down the street, who drove to services in a Cadillac, and laugh with my mother at the women's "Easter" hats she found so appalling. I know I once wanted to go to *shabbat* services with a junior high school friend, was excited and nervous, wondering what to wear, how to act, but the plans fell through somehow and I never passed beyond contempt and distance, never prayed or even watched others pray in the synagogue only two blocks from our apartment building. Perhaps not coincidentally, this same friend was one of the first teenage boys I showed my penis to, hoping he would reciprocate, but he didn't. This experience left me feeling stupid, weird, and worried that other kids would find out.

What *did* we observe in my family? We lit Chanukah candles (except on the days we forgot), and if my father did it, he said a prayer under his breath. My brother and I got the traditional Chanukah coins made out of chocolate. My parents each lit a *yorzeit licht,* a memorial candle, on Yom Kippur and on the anniversary of their parents' deaths. We ate "holiday dinners" somewhat fancier than the usual fare—to which dinners my father was invariably late from the store. But we never had a Passover Seder. I resisted the huge Workmen's Circle Seders because I knew I wouldn't feel at home there, and never went to a real one until I was twenty-six. Passover always embarrassed me, especially when friends asked what I did, where I'd gone.

I had no sense of Jewish holidays marking spiritual as well as historical time.

Partly because of my parents' very mixed feelings about being Jewish, and their professed superiority over observant Jews, I came to feel both estranged from more religious Jews and better than them—more rational and realistic, as if true observance were nonsense.

None of this seemed to matter until college, when I met and fell in love with Beverly Sheila Douglas—a tall, blonde, kind, lovely New Zealander. She was not Jewish.

I had dated girls erratically in junior high and high school, partly out of pressure to do so because everyone else was. I was attracted to these girls not as incarnations of femaleness, but as individuals. Each seemed ambivalent and maybe even frightened about dating and sex. Though we were physically affectionate, nothing seriously sexual ever happened between us.

In college I was pursued by "Bonnie," a smoldering theater major who had keys to the backstage dressing rooms. We met in one for a series of exciting winter afternoons in my sophomore year at Fordham University's Lincoln Center campus. We used my air force surplus coat as a blanket on the cold tile floor and it all seemed dreamlike to me, intensely pleasurable and confusing. How could this feel so natural when I was attracted to men?

I was nineteen then, and my brother had been asking me if I was still a virgin. I was determined not to be. And determined not to go to bed with a man, though I don't think I had the courage or insight to even articulate that taboo.

I met Beverly around the same time I was screwing with Bonnie, and broke off the relationship (if you could call it that) as Beverly and I started dating. We fell in love our junior year.

I had chosen a Catholic college because the campus was very small, my brother's Jewish girlfriend raved about her creative writing teacher there, and because it was Catholic. I'm sure of that now. I wasn't interested in converting, just hiding from Jewish identity, even though, as one of the very few Jews there, I actually stood out.

This turned out to be the first place I'd ever heard the phrase "jew him down" as a habitual part of people's conversation.

Beverly intrigued me because she was so different from American girls—softer, quieter. A Masterpiece Theatre junkie, I reveled in her anecdotes about England and New Zealand, her sophistication, her kindness. It never felt to me that I was faking our relationship, that I was Odysseus bound to the mast of his ship to keep from answering the sirens' call. I had never had any kind of sex with a boy or man; it was all so out of the realm of possibility. Yet I was always aware of attractive men in the street, and my secret must have been visible in my eyes because men occasionally tried to pick me up. As James Baldwin writes in *Another Country*, like all people with secret fantasies, my secret lived in my eyes "with all the brilliance and beauty and terror of desire."

The fact that Beverly wasn't Jewish didn't matter in the beginning. There was no conflict until we neared graduation and her visa was running out. It was time for couples to get married, or at least to become serious. Friends told us that Beverly and I were fun to watch and be with, and I suppose we did shine with the delicate snobbery of first love.

Friends bombarded me with what they thought about me and Beverly, what others thought, what I should think: a chorus, a babble deciding my life for me, or trying to help. Beverly, very English, could not talk about the future or her feelings; I, very scared and conflicted, could only stumble. I wanted to marry her, or maybe wanted not to lose her. Most of all, I wanted not to feel split and afraid of myself, afraid now of the feelings for men that lay coiled inside me like a snake ready to strike.

If my parents were aware of my struggle about marrying Beverly, they never brought it up, and I never raised it myself.

Several of our friends at Fordham were ostentatiously gay, bragging about their wild nights in the Village, at the bars, the docks, the trucks. These men who camped and dished with us must have known about me, but they loved Beverly and insisted we get married. They rooted for us.

I began feeling that Beverly's being a Christian did make a difference, and I was drawn to the Judaica section at Brentano's on Fifth Avenue. I bought books about Judaism and read them with more hunger than understanding, searching, I now realize, to find what being Jewish meant for me. I didn't know enough to decide. Just as I hesitantly bought gay books in junior and senior year, burying them in a stack of other paperbacks as if sheathing kryptonite with lead.

Christmas 1974 brought deeper discomfort. At a friend's house with Beverly, the tree decorating was fun, but hearing the host read from the New Testament seemed unnatural to me, embarrassing. The carols at the piano drove me down the hallway to another room. I didn't belong there; I knew it, felt it, believed it. This was not my holiday or my place. I had always been somewhat uncomfortable during New York's Christmas madness, but never so intensely. I told Beverly that. The presents under the tree I'd helped string lights and popcorn on were gifts of love, but ultimately not appropriate to whoever I suspected I was. The hostess and I had once disagreed about the possibilities of Jews being conscientious objectors. "Look at the Bible," she'd said. "It's full of violence." And I had then only secondhand words for reply, none of my own.

Beverly and I did not get married. I knew more and more clearly that I could not marry a non-Jew, no matter how much I loved her. What pushed me over the edge? Imagining Christmas, so profoundly a part of Beverly's life, in "our" house. I couldn't do it, nor could I ask her to give it up. I couldn't confuse myself or any children we might have. I wanted a Jewish home. No—it wasn't that affirmative. I realized I couldn't have a *non*-Jewish home; that was as far as I got, and it meant much more to me than my subterranean attraction to men. When I told Beverly I couldn't marry a non-Jew—painfully, reluctant to hurt her, but forced to the truth by her coming departure—I closed that religious door forever.

But I made a claim on part of my future.

When I returned from seeing Beverly off at Kennedy Airport (she was returning to New Zealand forever), I found a package on my desk at home. My first selection from the Jewish Book Club had come: a heavy one-volume encyclopedia of Judaica. I was too bitter to laugh, too stunned to cry.

My brother decided to marry the second-generation Polish Catholic he'd been dating for years, the woman he had said he would never marry, the woman my parents undoubtedly saw as "the enemy." Up at graduate school in Massachusetts, I received a phone call from him asking for help. Mom was "getting hysterical," crying. Dad was upset for her, for himself. My brother was stubborn, angry, and his girlfriend understandably incensed. If she was good enough to come to dinner and to live with him, then why—?

I made phone calls, wrote a frantic letter, said anything to keep what little family we had from destroying itself in bitterness and regret. It sounded like a catastrophe. I could imagine them getting married, my parents not coming, and me in the middle. I'm not sure how much I helped, but my parents calmed down because they had to. My brother would marry whomever he wanted, we all knew that, but the shock and resentment on all sides were inevitable. Later, I felt strangely betrayed. I had not married Beverly; how could my brother marry the woman he'd said he never would? I wished my brother hadn't taken something away from the family by marrying a non-Jew, but now I believe he had nothing to give. My brother was a Jewish Almanac Jew, the kind who likes knowing which movie stars changed their names.

I also felt bested by him, out-maneuvered in our unspoken rivalry. I couldn't count on marrying even a Jewish woman, and so even though my brother had dropped out of college, he was normal, and had just proven it in the most obvious way.

He'd told me about his wedding plans before my parents, and the impending crisis sent me to Yom Kippur services in Amherst, Massachusetts, to a steepleless white clapboard ex-church, unused to being the scene of Jewish prayer, where I sat in a crowded balcony, hardly comprehending the English of the *Mahzor* (holiday prayer book), but crying unexpectedly, moved by melodies I somehow knew, moved by the cantor's hall-filling eloquence, even by the children tramping on the stairs, moved by the fact that I was there, suffused by the beauty, the solemnity of group prayer for forgiveness, a publicly shared intimacy and hope.

I was roused and transfixed without understanding how or why, or what it all meant. I called home that night, to share my wonderment. My parents approved, just as they did next Passover when I didn't eat bread even though my matzo ran out. My parents might even have been proud, but like those who have stepped off a path, they could not fathom that I had felt the presence of a new possibility in my life.

It was my first synagogue service, my first Yom Kippur not listening to Kol Nidre on the radio or on a Jan Peerce album. I was twenty-three.

My brother's wedding, which took place in the United Nations chapel, was performed by a half-Jewish priest and a rabbi who looked Episcopalian. I held one pole of the *chupa,* the wedding canopy, and was thrilled by the ceremony, by the Hebrew that I did not understand. But the experience was odd for me. I was too uncertain in my own Jewish identity to condemn what my brother was doing—or to feel comfortable with it.

That year was traumatic for other reasons besides my brother's wedding. When I published my first short story, the event was overshadowed by my parents' severe reaction to it. This story had burst from me in a day and a half the year before, nursed by Kris, my writing teacher in college, who later became my closest friend. I read Kris the various sections over the phone as soon as they were finished, as if together we were tending a patient that might not recover. Her vigilance helped me begin to heal my own split from Judaism, because this story was about a child of Holocaust survivors who felt crushed by what he knew of his parents' terrible past. It won a prize and was published in *Redbook*.

It scared me.

When my parents read it, they felt betrayed and outraged at the way I'd woven in autobiographical elements. Even worse, my mother had weeks of insomnia, as well as gruesome nightmares about the war, feeling, no doubt, violated by the son she had hoped to protect from the brutal realities of her past—a son who had unwittingly led her back. When I tried talking about the story—which I stupidly withheld from them until it was published—she berated me as though I were not just her son but her persecutor, and she sneeringly tore the story apart. My father had little to say.

But the story led me to begin confronting my legacy as a child of survivors, and I started to read furiously about the Holocaust, steeping myself now in what had for years merely been bits of narrative gleaned from my parents, conquering my own nausea and fear of entering that Kingdom of Death. It was 1978, and Helen Epstein had made headlines with her book *Children of the Holocaust;* Holocaust curricula were being introduced all over the country; and Gerald Green's "Holocaust" had filled America's TV screens.

I was experiencing profound chaos in other ways. The night of my brother's bachelor party, I had left the Playboy Club, assaulted by its almost surreal heterosexuality to find a bar and get picked up.

That night was the fourth time I'd had sex with a man, and like the other times, it was colored by desperation, fear, and too much alcohol.

I ended up in a gay bar Beverly and I had visited twice to hear a comic singer who had mocked all the straight couples in the bar. "The guys always show up with a girlfriend first! Then they ditch her and come back alone." He was right about me. I had sat there with Beverly each time in a strange half-state, connected to her, in love, but hungering for the men around me and trying not to show it.

So, while my brother announced his marriage, I was enmeshed in a murkier, less public drama. At the University of Massachusetts, where I was doing an M.F.A. in creative writing, I was in love—or something—with one of my roommates in the house I shared at the edge of Amherst. "Scorpio" was of Italian descent: short, dark, heavy-shouldered, heavy-cocked, cynical. I had cast him in a dual role: He was my beloved, he was my tormentor. Always there, always out of reach. It was the kind of obsessive, confused, and unreal relationship you have with another man when you don't respect or understand your own homosexuality.

We never truly connected, we collided—with me usually feeling alternately bruised and elated. I would spend hours on the phone with friends trying to figure out what it all meant, as though I were struggling to turn lugubrious Derrida into crystalline and witty Jane Austen. My parents and my brother knew none of this, and I felt stranded. Unable to ask for what I wanted, unable to comprehend just what that was, I stumbled through a year of living in the same house with him, my changing moods a puzzle to our other housemates. Scorpio didn't really desire me at all, but wanted to put me in my place because I was the star writer in our creative writing program. An occasional fuck could do just that. At one party where my drunken dancing and enthusiasm galvanized the entire crowd, and attracted more than one woman, Scorpio got me away as soon as he could to prove in bed who was boss. These episodes sometimes seemed to occur in a parallel universe that we were only vaguely connected to.

The situation became even more tortuous and melodramatic when I wound up in bed with "Monica," a feisty, sharp-tongued, and grandly multiorgasmic woman who disliked Scorpio and had been actively pursuing me, promising me the love he could never offer. I tried to keep our affair secret from him. Monica was only the third woman I'd slept with, but our lovemaking was incredible and liberating. For the first time in my life, I felt relaxed in bed, free of inhibitions, criticism, fear. We made love by a waterfall out in the woods. We made love in the back of her Volkswagen station wagon, parked on the side of the road at night where headlights raked across us.

Because she had also slept with women (and considered herself an "ex-lesbian"), I never felt judged. But I felt trapped in what was almost a menage à trois, and the lying, the frustration, the tension all seemed to burst after the semester was over and I was back in New York. Away from Amherst, the situation seemed even more bizarre and confusing. Every phone conversation about it with Kris was like watching a wounded animal trying to drag itself to its feet: It stumbles, falls, stumbles again.

Wisely, Kris said I had to cut through everything, that we couldn't spend the rest of the summer this way, but I had to pull myself out, to go as far away as possible. This was the same friend who advised me in college that although I'd probably never meet a woman as kind as Beverly again (and she was right), it would not have made any sense to marry her when I felt uneasy about marrying a non-Jew and wondered if I was gay.

Now, in the summer of 1978, Kris asked, "Don't you have relatives in Israel?"

Hysterically eager to drop everything and run from my confusion, I announced to my parents that I would spend the coming year on a kibbutz. Alarmed by my vehemence, my parents suggested a few weeks just to see if I'd like it there, and I agreed. I called my uncle Wolf in Tel Aviv to let him know I was coming, and little more than a week later, I was gone—without telling Scorpio in advance, although Monica knew.

But the delight in leaving Scorpio behind me faded quickly. In my dark time, Israel was a bath of light, several rich, dense weeks of escape from a home that I hated to one I didn't know. Israel: stifling heat, long political discussions, bus rides, the unforgettable first vision of glowing Jerusalem, exploring Masada, surprising people with how much Hebrew I picked up, meeting my mother's brother Wolf for the first time, speaking Yiddish to his wife because her English was minimal. Israel: seeing a photo of my mother's other brother, the man whose name, Lev, I bore as Lewis, the man lost in the Battle of Stalingrad. Israel: a dream more real than the dream of America, older in the mind of God.

Yet even there I ran right into what I had fled. On a bright noisy hot street, I'd pass a truck whose driver was more beautiful than any man I'd ever seen. And spending a few days on a heartbreakingly scenic kibbutz on the Mediterranean, I ended up having sex with a Brazilian Jew who was even more withholding and uncommunicative than the man I'd left in Massachusetts. Despite the smooth skin and soft voice, he was not a kind man.

One night there, he fucked me and went off to shower, just assuming I'd come. Another night, after blowing and rimming him, I pushed up his heavy bronze-brown legs, but he shoved me away as soon as I entered him, claiming he was tired. Enraged, perplexed, I was unable to respond. In the morning, while he was gone, I contemplated ripping his clothes to shreds and destroying his few possessions.

Once more I was fleeing, this time back to Tel Aviv, where my puzzled uncle and aunt listened to my vague reasons for not staying at the kibbutz as long as I'd originally planned.

I returned to New York determined to change my name to Lev. Erica Jong writes in *Fear of Fifty*, "A name should be taken as an act

18

of liberation, of celebration, of intention. A name should be a magical invocation to the muse. A name should be a self-blessing."

I did all of that when I changed my name to Lev, liberating it from its Anglo-Saxon prison of "Lewis." Rocking one afternoon at my uncle's house, face-to-face with a picture of my mother, Wolf, and Lev, it had seemed dishonest to me to be named after Lev, yet not have his actual name. And the name Lev was a deepening of the link with my people and my history, because it had meanings in Yiddish (lion) and Hebrew (heart). Those languages even appear in the lives of Jews who don't speak or read them. Our religious and ritual terms are interchangeable, like *shabbos* (Yiddish) and *shabbat* (Hebrew).

I returned from Israel determined to speak Yiddish with my parents, to reclaim something of the past, and with a knowledge, undeveloped, unrefined, of the possibility of a deeper meaning to my life. Israel was another way, a different, difficult path, but far more rewarding, I thought, than graduate school. It was a life that could quench my thirst for meaning.

But I didn't take it. I had not even become a Jew—how could I become an Israeli?

The feelings of the Yom Kippur service in Amherst lay dormant for another two years. I was busy with finishing my degree, getting a part-time teaching job in New York at Fordham, my alma mater, writing and trying to get published, starting another degree, living at home again and reexperiencing why I'd wanted to leave: the coldness, the constriction. But I started subscribing to *Commentary*, which may seem laughable to some. For me, it was a big step to read *any* Jewish magazine. I chose it because it was the one I had heard most about. I learned a lot in its pages, and felt, however tenuously, more Jewish. I also felt repudiated for wanting men the day I read there Midge Dector's notorious homo-bashing essay "The

Boys on the Beach," a colorful diatribe about gay life on Fire Island and its threat to the American way of life.

I was so closeted at the time, and still relatively devoid of actual homosexual experience outside of reading, that the essay fascinated and excited me. It was like reading a foolish book review that convinces you to rush out and buy the book it's condemning. Despite the invective, you're dead sure that the reviewer is shortsighted and wrong. Midge Dector made me *long* for the life on Fire Island she found so disgusting. I'd had a similar reaction to *The Boys in the Band* when I saw it at fifteen. While as an adult I'm most struck by the self-hatred in that play, as a teenager I was flabbergasted at seeing gay men together—and encouraged. The movie told me that gay men were out there, real, alive; I wasn't alone.

Teaching at Fordham from 1978 to 1980 as an adjunct instructor, I had the opportunity of giving a "January Project," a course different from regular semester offerings. One fall night in 1979, it hit me: I would teach Holocaust literature. All that I'd read previously came back to me in a rush. I made a book list and syllabus, and plunged into three months of intensive research, reading even more than I had before, without stop: history, fiction, psychology, sociology, theology (I came across very few references to the situation of gays in the Holocaust). I was certain that literature had to be grounded in the reality it attempted to deal with, and in interpretations of that reality.

Children of Holocaust survivors tend to feel they know a lot about those nightmare years in Europe, given the way the Holocaust has left its imprint on their parents. But like many others, I actually knew little in the way of facts before I began reading, and came to see that I had wanted to know less because the Holocaust had stolen my parents' past not just from them but from me, and had made reminiscing a dangerous and bleak prospect. This drive to learn and teach was intimately bound up with my search for Jewishness.

The course—a difficult and intense month of readings, films, reports—surpassed any I'd ever done. Two-thirds Jewish, the students ventured along with me bravely, confused, awed, horrified, searching too. What did it mean? we all wondered. How could we think of it?

Midway, we read Tadeus Borowski's scorching collection *This Way for the Gas, Ladies and Gentlemen* and several of us had nightmares. Some students talked about dropping the class. One Catholic man said, "It hurts to read this—but why should it be easy?"

The most memorable student was a short hostile Jewish woman, initially contemptuous of what she called the Jews' "collaboration" in their death, who underwent a challenge of those beliefs and emerged so changed, so much more sensitive and tentative that we could all read the transformation in the very lines of her face. Another student, an older Polish man who had left Poland long before World War II, wrote in his journal about the troubling question of physical resistance: "It's very easy, sitting in a comfortable West End Avenue apartment, to talk about courage."

If anything, we all learned the extremity of conditions in the ghettos and camps, and found that New York standards of behavior did not, could not apply. And I emerged wondering if perhaps, as a son of Holocaust survivors, I hadn't found a *mission*. Traditional Jews observe 613 commandments; the philosopher Emil Fackenheim argues for a 614th after the Holocaust: to keep the memory alive. Perhaps that was what I could do. Teach others, give from my own special experience, transmit and interpret the past.

In that spirit, I wrote the first draft of the somewhat autobiographical novel that would be published twelve years later as *Winter Eyes*. The intense privacy and immersion, the sense of deepening my craft made me contemplate the role of my writing differently. It could serve a larger social purpose, as opposed to being my individual path to success. But neither writing nor teaching about the Holocaust would make me a Jew. One year later, I found out what could.

After seeing an advertisement in *Commentary*, I ordered a pamphlet from the American Jewish Committee about "ethnotherapy" for Jews, group therapy to help those who had absorbed cultural stereotypes about themselves. This little pamphlet unexpectedly ripped me open. The ugliness inside finally came to light: I realized that I had not one Jewish friend, that I hadn't seriously dated one Jewish girl, that I didn't particularly *like* Jews.

It was a revolution. I tore unread books from my shelves and plunged into them that week, submerged in discovery: Irving Howe's *The World of Our Fathers*, Cynthia Ozick's *The Pagan Rabbi*, Adin Steinsaltz's *The Essential Talmud*, the *Penguin Book of Jewish Short Stories*, a book on ancient Israel, and Milton Steinberg's *Basic Judaism*. That last, the most important, was a relic of my days with Beverly. I'd read it back then underlining everywhere, entering nowhere.

Now, I read slowly, absorbed, released from the slavery of false pride and ignorance. I loved this clear, concise little book: It seemed so wise to me and I knew then that Judaism, my religion of birth, could be my religion of choice. I loved the sensible way Steinberg discussed tradition and its modern application in every aspect of Jewish life.

It was a simple discovery to find that Judaism as a religion made sense, was even beautiful. Without having read about the death of European Jews, I don't think I could have understood or been able to appreciate their life, the tenets of a faith I'd known next to nothing about. And so, after feeling seared and overwhelmed by the horrors of 1933–45, I found myself in surprising harmony with my people's religion.

I was primed for still more discovery and change when I arrived at Michigan State University to pursue a Ph.D. the semester after teaching the Holocaust course. I gave a talk at the university's Jewish student foundation, Hillel, about Holocaust literature and had chosen that field for my dissertation, but something very different compelled me. My neighbor at the graduate dorm was Jewish and I accompanied him to what was only my second Yom Kippur service. I didn't fast—I wasn't ready to—but I achieved a nearness to prayer that now spurred a decision that rereading the pamphlet had made certain. Because I needed to be with Jews, I would move into MSU's Hillel co-op. I would live and eat and associate with Jews. What attracted me most about Hillel was not the well-stocked library but the small *shul* upstairs where an Orthodox congregation (*minyan*) met.

My *Commentary* subscription ran out and I ordered *Judaism* and *Midstream.*

Living with Jewish students was at first deeply unsettling for me. Did I fit in? Would I feel comfortable? As the routine took over, I realized we were as much students as Jews, maybe more so. This Jewish co-op turned out to be not very cooperative and not very Jewish. We did have one guy who was eternally vigilant and fanatical about kosher food, and some people attended Saturday morning services occasionally. Still, the Jewishness was one of concern for Israel and worry about anti-Semitism, a Jewishness of discussion and jokes, of atmosphere and self-parody. But then, none of the young men or women there was particularly in conflict about their Jewish identity or searching for ways to deepen it.

It was at services that I seemed to have found my pathway. The people there—Modern Orthodox—were relaxed and friendly, and one young couple began inviting me for *shabbat* lunch. Adina took me through the prayer book and explained what each prayer meant and what you did, and both she and Josh shared their learning in an easy, nonjudgmental way. They were witty, well-read, helpful.

My transitions were smooth. At one *shabbat* I donned a *tallis* (prayer shawl); at another I found myself swaying back and forth during the Amidah: *shokeling*. The service began to feel familiar and Hebrew stopped seeming completely foreign and forbidding. After many weeks, I began joining in some of the sung prayers. I began lighting candles on Friday night. I started wearing a *kipa* (yarmulkah) when I read from a *siddur* (prayer book) or *chumash* (Pentateuch with commentary) outside of services. I kissed the holy books when I closed them (as Orthodox Jews do) not because I thought I should but because I chose to acknowledge them as sacred and because the act itself felt beautiful. The impulse came from deep inside, where a sense of reverence was growing. Each service I attended gave me more understanding, beauty, more belief, and connection. Prayer, once foreign and contemptible, enriched my life. Even when I was bored or tired, being there was the Jewish immersion I had not known I craved.

I had never bothered learning my full Hebrew name until that year in the co-op. I was a *Levi*, my father told me: *Reuven Lev ben Shlomo ha-Levi*. Because *Levi*s are supposedly descended from Temple functionaries who sang the psalm of the day, among other duties, this name connected me to centuries of Jews. Up at the *bima* (lectern), saying the Torah blessings, I felt the march of Jewish time, and felt myself a part of it. Perhaps most profoundly, one Yom Kippur, the first on which I fasted, I held the Torah while the plangent Kol Nidre was chanted. It was ineffably moving to me, and that evening I had a dream in which a warm voice sang the words *Av Harachamim*, Father of Mercy. The dream told me that I was welcomed and embraced.

Almost every week, I read the Torah portion in advance, or while it was being chanted, and plunged into the footnotes, feeling very much like a sort of feral child. Why had all this information about Jewish faith and observance been kept from me? And would I ever come to feel knowledgeable, truly at ease among worshiping Jews?

Mordechai Nisan, a visiting scholar from Israel, lodged in Hillel's guest room one weekend and dined with the co-op members. He spoke movingly that *shabbat* afternoon about *shabbat* in Israel involving everyone and being a different kind of time. As he spoke, I thought of the *shabbat* prayer: "Be pleased with our rest." At lunch I'd told him about my background, or lack of it. Stumbling through *Birkat HaMazon* (the sung and chanted prayers after meals), I felt him considering me. When he left, he said, "I hope you find what you're looking for."

But he didn't know that there was another hunger in me, as deep as my need to belong and fit in as a Jew. If I were a teenager in the mid-nineties, I'm not sure I would ever seriously date a woman, but given the times and my own conflicts, in the early eighties, I continued to date and enjoy my relationships with women (though the countervailing attraction to men never disappeared).

I found some brief resolution in considering myself bisexual, and there was a great deal of popular literature at the time to give me some ballast.

Moving into Hillel's co-ed co-op, I was thrown together far more intimately with men than I was at the dorm. Rather than sharing a bathroom with one guy, I shared it with several. One of them had an enormous penis and joked about it as often as he could, eyeing me to see what my reaction was. Another became the model for "Eric" in my story "Shouts of Joy." One student talked about his intense camping trips with his "old buddy" and made references to a bisexual woman friend, possibly as unconscious signals. I felt somewhat besieged and afraid of exposure, both enjoying and fearing the random displays of nudity in the men's room, further heightened when someone's friend or boyfriend slept over.

After living in the co-op for a year, I moved out and into my first apartment, but still went to services and events at Hillel. The physical distance was matched by my burgeoning discomfort with Orthodox restrictions on women. Once I overcame the newness and excitement of being part of a prayer community, I felt increasingly uncomfortable with what I saw as the lesser role of women in an Orthodox service—and of my own exclusion if I were openly gay.

Josh and Adina once mentioned a congregation they knew where a lesbian had been asked to leave when she came out. I found myself agreeing that it was "a shame," but tried to cover my disappointment when they went on to remark that the woman shouldn't have embarrassed her synagogue in that way. This anecdote told to me in 1981 eventually inspired my story "Dancing on Tisha B'Av," but at the time it was more admonishing than inspiring. The lines were clearly drawn for me. I had to keep part of myself hidden.

Yet it was being grounded in a profoundly, unequivocally Jewish milieu that brought me real depth and success as a writer. After the shock of being published at twenty-four, and my parents' violent reaction to the story, I kept writing, but somehow never wrote anything as good as that prize-winning story. It began to haunt me—what if I were like some character in a Hawthorne tale, doomed to be endlessly dissatisfied after the first taste of achievement? But in 1983, the drought ended. In Michigan, I'd begun reassessing my writing, wondering what I truly had to say and who my audience was. It was easier there to disconnect from New York ideas of success and to decide that being in *The New Yorker* or other national magazines wasn't the only way to find satisfaction as a writer.

I started sending my work to Jewish publications, and the response was swift and amazing. Stories of mine, mostly about children of survivors, began appearing in Jewish magazines and newspapers. Editors loved my work, and so apparently did readers. Now I had an audience and a new sense of mission. For the first time in my writing career, I was thinking less of the glory of being published and much more about reaching people. But my success as a Jewish writer ironically drove me further into the closet. Having finally come to feel comfortable and accepted as a Jew, and established as a published writer, how could I risk either of those achievements by coming out? Especially in a city like East Lansing, whose Jewish community was so small?

Still deeply uncertain about being gay, and at the point where I was finally comfortable in my new Jewish affiliation, I unexpectedly fell in love with a Jewish man I met at the university. Unfortunately, he was married, with children. His research and writing about shame gave me a whole new set of insights about my past, my relationship to my parents, my Jewishness, my homosexuality. I felt the promise of freedom.

There were uncanny similarities in our backgrounds—we went to the same high school in New York, our fathers were in the same business—and it wasn't long before we acknowledged that we were soul mates. You could see it in the way we taught and wrote together. He and I would finish each other's sentences in class or as we worked on a piece of writing. Gersh is not a child of survivors, but he is the son of Eastern European immigrants, and we share a cultural landscape through which we move with ease and recognition together.

Our deepening bond transformed both our lives. Gersh was the first to know clearly what he wanted, and that meant pain for himself and his family at the time. Gersh wanted a life together with me, and felt our meeting was *besherit* (fated)—but I couldn't imagine the possibility. I had never met a committed gay couple, let alone a Jewish one. It took several more years and great pain for us both until I could come to terms at last with what we meant to each other, to finally make a lifetime commitment.

Of course, as we worked all of this out, I withdrew even further from the Jewish community in East Lansing, after having a bar mitzvah at the age of thirty in Hillel's other, egalitarian minyan.

My bar mitzvah marked my confidence and sense of belonging as much as it was a temporary farewell.

My Jewish journey was additionally complicated in the 1980s by Gersh's own problems with his Jewish background. His parents forced an unexplained and insensitive Orthodoxy on him from an early age, and our praying together only partially healed his pain and sense of separation from other Jews.

While I drew back from East Lansing's Jewish world, Gersh and I continued to teach and write together as we struggled with coming out. Our lives grew richer through the courses we codeveloped and co-taught at Michigan State University; the books and articles we wrote together (as well as separately, with each other's guidance); and the many students we reached. The deepening of our love and commitment taught me the reality of that *shabbat* hymn, *kol ho-olam kulo:* "All of life is a narrow bridge, the important thing is not to be afraid." Just as my writing was beginning to include gay as well as Jewish themes, we bought a house and moved in together, and that move gave me great courage. I was no longer afraid to publish fiction in my own name in a gay publication; I welcomed having my story "Dancing on Tisha B'Av" appear in George Stambolian's *Men on Men 2* in 1988. Meeting people in San Francisco or Provincetown who had read my work or recognized my name, I felt more settled and comfortable as a gay man, as a gay writer.

By 1990, I made a giant leap forward by proudly and unambivalently publishing *Dancing on Tisha B'Av*, a book of Jewish and gay short stories that was advertised as such—a book full of as many connections as contradictions. What is the role of gays and lesbians in American Jewish life? How can their dual identities be reconciled? How do children of Holocaust survivors find meaning in their parents' lives? The questions this book raised had personal relevance for me, but also larger and current social implications.

Until that point, coming out as a gay man seemed to overshadow coming out as a Jew—but no longer. At the first national

gay and lesbian writers' conference in San Francisco in 1990, I not
only spoke to four hundred people about coming out in my writing as a Jew and a gay man, but I had a pivotal encounter with the
writer Jyl Lynn Felman, whom I had not seen in ten years. She had
been in my M.F.A. writing program, at a time when neither one of
us was out of the closet. When she shared her journey with me as a
deeply-committed Jewish lesbian (who also had a Jewish partner), I
was electrified and stirred to action. That conference, which drew
1,200 people, opened me up for another one that was unexpectedly
even more fulfilling.

Gersh and I attended the 1990 Midwest Regional Meeting of
the World Congress of Gay and Lesbian Jewish Organizations, in
Toronto. The experience was truly an answer to our prayers. There
were *shabbat* services led by a gay rabbi, in which the *siddur* (prayer
book) recognized and included the experience of gay and lesbian
Jews—most movingly, perhaps, before the Kaddish, when we re-
flected on those who had never had Kaddish (the prayer for the
dead) said for them, and on those who had died with their true
selves hidden. It was there, at that *erev shabbat* that Gersh and I felt
completely ourselves, completely embraced by thousands of years
of Jewish tradition and worship. That weekend there were semi-
nars, meetings, shmoozing (and cruising), another powerful *shabbat*
service, and an overwhelming tour of Toronto's Holocaust museum.
But the culmination for me was a final dinner, where our table of
ten was laden with Yiddish speakers with whom I shared jokes and
songs after we sang *Birkat HaMazon,* the grace after meals. My old
world and my new world were united, joyously.

Since that time, we have attended World Congress meetings in
London, San Francisco, Detroit, and Tel Aviv, appearing on the
program in each city. Gersh is the foremost theorist and writer in
the U.S. on the emotion of shame, and his workshops have dealt
with the intersections of shame with both gay and Jewish identity.
I have talked about coming out as a Jew and a gay man and claim-

ing both identities, and have read from my fiction. For both of us, these conferences have been an opportunity to give back to our community of lesbian and gay Jews, to offer what we know most deeply, by way of thanks, because we feel so nourished and connected.

Encouraged by Reform Judaism's efforts to make a place for lesbian and gay Jews, Gersh and I joined our local Reform synagogue as an openly gay couple. Three times now, I have led the synagogue's Holocaust Remembrance Day service. The second time, it was a service I had written and compiled, which included homosexuals among the list of Nazi victims.

Gersh and I also belong to a Detroit-area gay and lesbian Jewish group called Simcha (joy), whose services we find far more meaningful than those at our Reform synagogue because they include lesbian and gay experience, and because the group is more intimate and friendly. Being there stills the longing for the closeness and warmth I first felt in the Orthodox minyan (even though I have never been by any stretch of the imagination an "Orthodox Jew"). Gersh and I are integral parts of Simcha, and our closest Jewish friends are there. It's in our involvement with this group and other gay Jewish groups around the country that I feel most committedly Jewish. My extensive reading tour after *Dancing on Tisha B'Av* was published concentrated as much on gay Jewish groups as bookstores, because I felt *this* was my primary audience.

I have seen that my work is helping encourage other Jewish gay writers to combine both sides of their life in their writing. There's a rich body of work by Jewish lesbians, but far less writing by Jewish gay men; hopefully my work can contribute to the growth of the men's literature. This sense of mission is like what I felt in the late seventies when I contemplated teaching and writing about the Holocaust. But the present mission is based on a deeper and calmer vision. It's truly social action in the Jewish sense of *tikkun olam*, repairing the world.

I'm not remotely as observant as I was when I was attending the Orthodox minyan at Michigan State, and I do sometimes miss the sense of excitement and immersion in ritual I had then. But I've also learned to accept the fluctuations in my own need to be involved in Jewish activities and rituals.

One of the most moving injunctions in the Torah is that "the stranger in your midst shall be as the native. For remember, once you were a stranger in the land of Egypt." This call is a central part of every Passover Seder. Alienated for so long from other Jews, deeply divided about my own homosexuality, I have felt myself twice strange: Jewish in the gay community, gay in the Jewish community. In each, different, lesser, ashamed. But living with and loving a Jewish man, exploring our Jewishness and gayness together, have made it possible for me to exceed what Evelyn Torton Beck has called "the limits of what was permitted to the marginal." Coming out as a Jew ultimately made it possible for me to come out as a gay man and then work at uniting the two identities. As Beck puts it so beautifully in *Nice Jewish Girls,* the "experience of being outside the bounds of society" as a Jew made me "more willing to acknowledge other ways in which [I stood] outside."

It was almost twenty years ago that I started exploring my Jewish past and wondering about a Jewish future. That search has been inevitably interwoven with coming out and finding love. In that dual journey, writing has been both a catalyst and a laboratory for change. Having just passed my seventeenth year as a published writer and my forty-first birthday, I feel the surprise and joy Lena does in *Light in August* when she says, "My, my. A body does get around."

Okemos, Michigan

2

Okemos, Michigan

We were just looking—that's all I had agreed to.

Ten years ago, I had reluctantly said I would "look," after Gersh had called while I was at a conference in San Francisco. He told me that we should buy a house in Okemos (where we had separate apartments) instead of trying to rent one, because there weren't many rentals available just then in Okemos, near East Lansing. I felt both sick and stunned at the idea of owning a house, let alone our actually living together, and the day after he called, I came down with the flu.

I had grown up in Washington Heights, a hilly and park-filled upper Manhattan neighborhood as remote to many New Yorkers as Riverdale or even Albany, though it's now infamous for the cocaine sales and murders scarring its shaded boulevards and Depression-era buildings. Back then, I thought of houses as completely alien, out in the suburbs, something to visit or drive by. And I pictured them as negatively as Birkin did in *Women in Love:* "'the world all in couples, each in its own little house, watching its own little interests, and stewing in its own little privacy—it's the most repulsive thing on earth.'"

But Indian Hills, the Okemos subdivision in which we looked

at a third house one sunny May morning, was not at all repulsive. It is an oak-lined neighborhood of about two hundred houses, a few miles from Michigan State University in East Lansing, with curving streets; old blue spruces, maples, scotch pines, towering arbor vitae, weeping willows, and magnolias; overgrown yew hedges and shrubs; lots of nearly an acre; and thirty- or forty-year-old houses set well back from the road. While there are some large homes, this is not the wealthiest part of a prosperous and stoutly Republican suburb studded with Michigan State faculty members, but dominated by Lansing-area professionals whose wives wear mink and drive Cutlass Cierras, Jaguars, and an occasional Porsche. The houses in Indian Hills are not at all pretentious, like the newer, Tudoresque homes in nearby subdivisions that dwarf their tiny lots.

Indian Hills is even more appealing given that a few minutes away you could be in any featureless part of the homogenized Midwest, swamped by malls and mini-malls, wholesale outlets, fast food and video encampments, and grim acres of parking lots. Best of all, the day we saw our house, we drove off East Lansing's and Okemos's main street, Grand River Avenue, to cross a narrow bridge into the subdivision. The road curved around the neighborhood's nine-hole golf course, which was studded with groups of shirtless hunky young MSU students as picturesque as classical statuary on an English lord's estate. "Beautiful," I murmured. And it all was, though the four-bedroom house we stopped at looked like a simple ranch from outside. It was fronted at the street by a ginkgo tree, which I recognized from its fan-shaped leaves because one had grown in the park near my elementary school in Inwood. Finding the ginkgo and having crossed the bridge made me feel I had entered some childhood fantasy.

Nearer the house was an enormous flowering tree in full bloom, whose wide-spreading boughs started from just a few feet above the ground; the blossoms were fuschia, edged with white. I discovered it was a hawthorn, the first one I had ever had pointed out to me, and so, like a child learning the word *table,* I felt suddenly possessed of mysterious but useful information.

Years before this morning, in New York, I had gone apartment hunting with my college writing teacher and best friend Kris, and we had unexpectedly and angrily fled from one with a sumptuous view of the Hudson because the apartment made us feel very anxious. "This is an *awful* place," Kris said, confused by the intensity of her feeling. "Something *terrible* happened here!" It did feel awful, almost possessed, but this house on Chippewa Drive in Okemos felt welcoming and warm. From a brick-walled vestibule, we stepped into a large open living room/dining room (the "great room") with a stone fireplace at one end. The long wall with large windows facing the back was not parallel to the one opposite it, and neither was a wall in the dining area, yet somehow these anomalies were delightful.

Gersh and I looked at each other, and kept looking as we moved through the house, which was bigger and deeper than it had seemed from the street, and far more beautiful. The colors throughout were royal blue, maroon, beige, and orange, and kept appearing in varying combinations in shades, curtains, custom-made rugs. Our tiny, tipsy-sounding realtor with big hair explained it was a "red-ribbon house"—you could move right in without having to change or prepare anything. That expression made me think of a contest capped by prizes and applause.

Each room drew us into the next. Details kept bursting on us like fireworks: the Italian tiles in the kitchen, exquisite fabric on the living room walls, honey-colored pine in the room I knew would be my study because it faced that glorious hawthorn in the front yard. We were falling in love not just with the house, but with the *idea* of ourselves there, with the idea of a home. We fit in. We looked at it twice more that day, brought Gersh's two sons over to see what they thought (since they would be spending about half their time with us), we looked at each other and said yes, and we made our offer that evening.

Gersh had wanted to live with me for years, but I had never believed it was possible—not because I doubted that gay men could live loving and happy lives together, but partly because Michigan, and more particularly the East Lansing area, had already become my home as an outwardly straight man, and I was unprepared to make the shift, to emerge, to give up my "anonymity." I had come to Michigan in 1981 ostensibly to do a doctorate, but really to escape my family, and, more important, to escape New York. It was a city I no longer had the courage or patience to live in: dirtier, noisier, more crowded and dangerous than the city I had assumed was the center of the universe when I was growing up. Two and a half years in bucolic Amherst, Massachusetts, had shown me I could flourish outside New York.

I fell in love with Michigan when I got here, exploring MSU's lush and spreading campus, traveling around the state with its more than three thousand miles of Great Lakes shoreline, up to Hemingway country, to Lake Michigan, Lake Huron, the Keweenaw peninsula, crossing the Mackinac (pronounced Mackinaw) Bridge at sunset. Life seemed simpler here, less oppressive, more inviting; like Joni Mitchell's free man in Paris, here in Michigan, "I felt unfettered and alive." Of course, being a graduate student is a strange mix in which the elements of servitude are often masked by romanticism, but even as I was finishing my degree, I knew that I would want to stay here: People were friendlier and more relaxed, without the defensive "walls" that most cities demand for survival. And most importantly, I could write here. In the mid-eighties, I had finally begun to feel that I had a career as a writer, and an audience.

Gersh was also a transplanted New Yorker (we had gone to the same high school, ten years apart) and felt about Michigan as I did. But having already made his great plunge into the future through divorce, he was ready and eager for a complete life together. The most I had previously agreed to was getting an apartment in the same complex he lived in. No one would see us, I thought. And here was the other side of living in Okemos: visibility. There were no crowds to lose yourself in. So, this sudden about-face, the abruptness of my decision to say yes to the house, to our living together, was all the more astonishing for both of us.

When we finally moved into the house, I was paranoid about being observed every time we were out in the enormous backyard with its two sassafras trees, sugar maples, and red oaks, or trimming hedges in the front, or even walking to the front door with groceries. In New York, neighbors had seemed tamer, less intrusive, even though they were sometimes just on the other side of a wall. You chatted with them in elevators or lobbies, at the mailboxes, but their scrutiny was something I rarely thought of. Here, I felt exposed and vulnerable, and it didn't help that every year when Gay Pride day came along, letters in MSU's student newspaper and the *Lansing State Journal* condemned homosexuality with unswerving hatred that masked itself as Christian love and salvation. Gersh tried to calm my anxieties with jokes, but it turned out that I was right. We *were* being watched, although not in the way I had imagined.

As we began shaping the house to become our own, we started a series of changes that kept escalating like those five-year plans in the former Soviet Union. After fruitless attempts to trim back the overgrown yews that hulked at practically every corner of the house, we started having them removed. Then we began replanting. My world expanded as we became habitués of local greenhouses and entered a community of gardeners. Each conversation I had about soil conditions, or sunlight, pests, drought stress, or winter kill marked how different this world was for me. I began to worry about how certain shrubs were doing, consulting books and experts. Plants became a permanent and enjoyable part of my conversation as I began to feel at home with them, and with the soil under my fingernails after an afternoon of planting.

The new and more interesting evergreens we planted at the front of the house, under the study window in a raised, stoned-edged bed, got our neighbors' attention. On either side of us and across the street lived elderly men and women, and all remarked on how well we were taking care of the house, especially that we were raking the leaves in the fall and not letting them scatter onto someone else's lawn. The lawn itself was a frequent subject of conversation. The previous owners had left it alone, which meant in the summer it was seared, thin, brown, and the rest of the year not much better, but we hired a lawn care firm and then installed an underground sprinkling system. People walking by on a nice day, from several streets over, would remark on the lovely changes in the property. They *had* been watching. And I realized I did the same. As we drove into or out of Indian Hills, I found myself intensely aware of changes in people's yards, new plantings, remodelings, and problems with a tree or shrub. I was becoming deeply connected to this place.

We also began changes in the house itself. And each alteration—whether it was new locks, a French door between the vestibule and the living room, or the entirely remodeled master bathroom and new roof—had the effect of making me feel more stable, more rooted, more secure. All of this was as exciting as working outdoors on the trees and shrubs because I had always lived in rental apartments, which stayed essentially the same no matter how creatively I moved my furniture around.

The greatest change was adding a deck onto what had been a scruffy screen porch, and having the porch itself enclosed, heated, and made into a sunroom. The large windows let in the outside, but also made the house more open. I was growing less afraid of that, after we had taken out the grim chain-link fence the previous owners kept because of their dogs. This whole experience was a profound new reality for me. In just two years we had stripped the house bare of its ugly, obscuring yews, and opened up the backyard to the unexpected: a dog wandering through, utility repairmen up on their poles, the glances of strangers in other yards.

This was *my* house. I could do what I wanted. I could be what I wanted. If we hugged or held hands on the deck, it was our business and no one else's. Owning a house and creating a home had the entirely unexpected effect of making me gradually more proud, aggressive, more determined to be "out," to overcome the years of silence and lies. I see now that living in an apartment, or even renting a home would have continued the climate of hiding because the front door opens into transience. Here, I felt committed to living in this place, to voting for a board of supervisors that would slow the rate of growth in our township, to signing petitions about road closures or recycling, to writing letters to local officials so that my voice would be heard. I cared about the environment in this beautiful neighborhood—so quiet you could always hear the mourning doves or the chickadees—in ways I never could have cared in New York because someone else would be responsible there, surely.

If I had previously felt suspicious or hostile toward the idea of living in a house, perhaps part of what fueled my distance was the inevitable image of children. With only a few isolated moments of longing, I had never wanted to be a father, yet that's what I became when we moved in together, because Gersh shared custody of his two sons with his ex-wife, who lives a few minutes away. He was determined to stay in Okemos after his divorce so that he could be near his boys and so they could easily travel to and from school from either parent's home with minimum disruption. Both boys knew me and seemed to like me, but the bonds that developed between us when we started to live together became as powerful as my connection to the physical in my environment.

In the past ten years, my sense of time has shifted radically, and

I am much more attuned to the seasons, as well as to the stages of a life. I eagerly note the first crocuses of spring and feel comforted by the smell of burning leaves in the fall, just as I've been aware of the boys getting taller, filling out, leaving the whining of childhood behind for the testing of adolescence, the burdens of young adulthood.

It was David, the elder boy, who at fourteen started talking about doing things "as a family"—a term that Gersh and I were determined not to force on him or Aaron, his younger brother. David wanted to go out to eat, all four of us, and to play board games and card games, especially ones he was good at. Many nights we played hours of hearts, and as with any family, each game recalled wild jokes and terrific plays of previous games. It was clear to me that we were building a history together.

Gradually, I was drawn into the boys' lives, and have become an acknowledged "third parent" for them. It started with my helping with their homework, especially their writing assignments, and then running errands for them or with them—to their mother's house, to the mall, into town, to a friend's, or just going for a ride. Having another adult in the house made parenting a lot easier for Gersh, because he didn't have to be the only one the kids relied on. Having "backup" has been particularly valuable in family arguments because we can break down into teams, and someone always seems to be reasonable and in control, able to act as a sounding board.

Each year has brought new levels of closeness, as with David telling me things he asks me not to share with his father, or coming in after school and chatting about his day. He has told me that those chats have been the high point of each day, a chance for the two of us to get to know each other outside of the constraints of the group. Aaron and I have gone out by ourselves to see movies or shop, and my feelings for the boys have been a surprise. Talking to people who don't know me, I often reply to a comment about their children with, "Yes, my son does that too." The first time I mentioned this to the boys, they seemed very pleased. They can't have been too surprised, though, because we've all shared a great deal in ten years. We've had season tickets for the football team, and even went out to the Rose Bowl in 1988 when Michigan State was the Big Ten champion (and beat USC!). We have taken short trips together, seen rock concerts, plays, and musicals at MSU's concert hall and elsewhere, gone on college visits, and Gersh and I have helped with their writing for school and on applications.

There have been other, unexpected connections between us.

Two years ago, Gersh and I went to a Rosh Hashanah service partly led by Aaron. It had been a year of explosive growth for Aaron as a Jew. The catalysts were his deep involvement with the Greater Lansing Temple Youth, his attendance at several statewide conclaves for Jewish youth, and his time at the national Jewish leadership academy. Aaron was wondering what God meant to him, finding his place as a Jew, and not least, learning the guitar to be a song leader. His father and I marveled at his maturity and thoughtfulness in this search.

Gersh and I and about thirty others, mostly teenagers, attended a one-hour Rosh Hashanah service at our synagogue, and it was far more than we had anticipated: dynamic, moving, passionate, and personal.

Instead of a stage and an enormous hall, there was a small disheveled classroom decorated with travel posters for Israel, and an aleph bet chart. Instead of hundreds of people, many bored and chatting, there were only dozens, all singing and intent. Instead of distance, there was intimacy. The "creative service" started with a story about a simple shepherd who couldn't pray, but offered up his music to God. That is what I felt we were doing. The melodies of the prayers—many by the innovative Jewish writer Debbie Friedman—were warm and embracing, and often on the point of tears, I felt the transcendence that I hope to feel at services, but seldom experience except at nontraditional Jewish groups like Simcha, the Detroit-area organization for Jewish gays and lesbians Gersh and I belong to. Even more, the story of the shepherd, for me, included all those Jews who either don't have the Jewish education to feel fully comfortable at a service, and those who feel, as I did that morning, the futility of words.

I was incredibly proud of Aaron, who led services with the other guitar players as if he had been doing so for years. He was confident, smooth, relaxed, and smiling, his eyes connecting with those in the room again and again, his voice blending skillfully with the other two song leaders. His father and I were aglow with pride in Aaron's Jewish commitment and his newfound talent.

Afterward, I told Aaron what a gift he had, and how this service had connected my heart and my head. And in words my mother would have used, I told him that he surely had a *"yiddishe neshomah,"* a Jewish spirit.

All the parents attending were similarly moved and delighted. One commented, "That was the Jewish future in there."

Melodies from the service drifted through my head the rest of the day, and I felt at peace. It was totally unexpected, but completely welcome because I had come to the service in deep pain.

Almost a year before, my mother sunk into paranoia, terrifying confusion and violence that could only be controlled by heavy doses of drugs that left her quietly smiling and inoffensive. I wondered who was really there now behind the chemical wall that doctors felt was the only response to her multi-infarct dementia, a stroke-caused disease that looks very much like Alzheimer's. Off drugs today, my mother no longer recognizes anyone, never speaks, and is barely present. My father was inconsolable, my brother and I stunned, despairing.

Sitting in our temple on the eve of Rosh Hashanah (the day before we attended the service Aaron led), I rebelled as soon as I opened up *Gates of Repentance* and read about God's power and mercy.

Mercy?! How could God be called merciful when my mother had suffered through the unspeakable agonies of concentration camps, and was now deprived of her sense, cut off from her husband of almost forty years, from her children, from herself? I felt bitter, restless, incensed. The service felt like an unscalable cliff wall. God seemed intolerably far from me that night, and I felt the past was bearing down on me. Driving away later, I knew that these were age-old feelings and questions, but the continuity of doubt and pain did not console me.

And then the next morning—unexpectedly—I felt healed, thanks largely to Aaron and his music.

Having two children living with us, and feeling ourselves a family, has also unexpectedly helped ground me in the reality of my own identity as a gay man. I have found myself explaining news items to the kids about gay rights, sharing my outrage over Jesse Helms and other troglodytes—in other words, letting them know what moves and alarms me. I am a news addict, and both boys have become used to watching the evening news and talking about it, asking questions. David's intense interest in current events led to his majoring in international relations at the University of Wisconsin at Madison, then spending a year abroad at the University of Warwick in England. Aaron's social consciousness has expressed itself in deep involvement with environmental activities at his high school.

Living with people who love me has had the effect of making my freedom at home more precious, and the public opprobrium gays and lesbians deal with every day more pernicious. Gersh and I are not shy about being affectionate with each other, nor do we keep our involvement in gay causes secret. If anything, we have been convinced that modeling a healthy, committed, and politically aware and active relationship between two men is crucial.

How we live has the potential to be a message to the boys that will hopefully override the sick and destructive messages about gays that they are bombarded with by their peers and by our culture.

The sense of security and family we feel has propelled us into an unexpected series of activities. Gersh and I were founding members of a study group of faculty and staff at Michigan State University that met regularly with the aim of establishing a gay and lesbian studies program at the university. We were also founding members of a Lansing-area coalition of gay and lesbian groups meeting to bridge the various gaps between the two communities and to develop joint political action. Both groups have convened at our house on various occasions, and the kids were well-informed of their aims. Gersh has offered a workshop at MSU's Counseling Center on self-esteem for gay men, and has codeveloped and co-taught Michigan State's first course in gay and lesbian studies. We are both committed to making Lansing and Michigan more open, more accepting, and more protective of lesbians and gay men—because this is our home, and we cannot accept anything less. That has led to many letters and editorials for our campus paper, for the *Detroit Jewish News*, and the *Lansing State Journal.*

When Gersh and I first met, marveling at how much we had in common, our home was the world of ideas, because we started writing articles and then a book together. Everything we have co-authored has been published, and our joint teaching and lecturing has likewise been as powerful for our students and audiences as for us—knitting us together, creating a world of shared experiences. All of that laid a foundation for living together and ultimately making Okemos prove to us what Elizabeth Bowen says in her novel *The Death of the Heart,* that "home is where we emotionally live."

Letter from Israel, I

3

Letter from Israel, I

I

The sun seemed to burn all sound off the long slow waves licking and foaming in pantomime. I sat far back from the water, staring. Tomorrow, my third day at a kibbutz on the Mediterranean, I would no longer be a "guest of the kibbutz." After sunrise, I would start painting newly built apartments. I had spent just a week in Israel, staying with an aunt and uncle outside Tel Aviv. I'd toured Jerusalem, the Negev, Caesaria, Masada, the Dead Sea. For now, my traveling was over.

Somewhere behind me I heard the thick guttural voices of the Dutch women. Most of the kibbutz volunteers were from the Netherlands or Scandinavia; they had come as soon as the Yom Kippur War of 1973–74 was over, and had stayed on. Two large Swedish women lived in the tin-roofed shack next to mine. They did peculiar calisthenics out in front, eyeing me with clinical disapproval whenever I passed. I was so skinny and undeveloped. Many of the volunteers spoke English, as did the kibbutzniks, but I had not come to Israel to talk, or to think.

I stroked sand from my thighs, picked up my towel, and made

my way up the slope to the kibbutz's well-planted cliff line. In my small damp room, I sank onto the battered cot to nap before dinner, but my roommate Roberto, a Brazilian Jew, came in from the showers and took a long time drying his red-brown body. I squeezed my eyes shut. Slim, boyish, incongruously blue-eyed, he had the poignant dark perfection of an angel in a Renaissance fresco, from dense Botticelli curls to slim, incredibly high-arched and delicate feet.

The night before, he had invited me to walk on the beach: "The moon . . ." he sighed. But I had read on in the Jane Austen paperback I'd bought in Tel Aviv, reassured by the book's rhythms, which cooled me more than the jerky little shelf fan could. At night, the shack's walls, grimy with abandoned posters, snapshots, and a crumbling papier-mâché mask were not so lonely to look at. The unfamiliar sea whisper almost convinced me I was getting somewhere.

I had abruptly fled the meltdown of a messy menage à trois in bucolic western Massachusetts for ten days in Israel. As a child of concentration camp survivors, I had family nowhere else in the world, so Israel was the one destination for which I could make a call, buy a ticket, and leave within a week of the slightly hysterical decision—knowing I'd find some kind of home when I got there.

And Israel was far enough away for me to feel a vicious sense of satisfaction when I sent a postcard from the airport to the man in Massachusetts who was driving me crazy: *Going to Israel.* I wanted to be unreachable, but I also wanted to feel safe.

I did. Safe, and absent. Everything in Israel seemed simpler, reduced to fundamentals: heat, sun, dust, crowds, Hebrew, surcease.

I had gotten off at the wrong bus stop for this kibbutz, and had to walk miles along a featureless dusty road until an army officer gave me a lift. On my hike, I was exhilarated by the thought that there was no one in the world who knew where I was. I had truly escaped.

After dinner on my second night, Roberto asked me again if I felt like a moonlit walk as we left the large high-raftered dining hall. We passed the charming members' area where each balconied little building was fronted by a luxuriant garden. Below and beyond the crescent slope spread the sea, folding over its own darkness.

Roberto pointed at the full moon and I looked up.

"Well *I* will take a walk, then," he said, moving away to a patch that led down and down again to the beach, his yellow T-shirt and skimpy white shorts vivid against the night. I trailed back to my cot. The room stank of damp and darkness, and, lying down, I could only picture him barefoot on the sand.

I got up, took my key to lock the door behind me, and headed down the nearest path to the beach, slowly. Far up the coast the lights of Haifa broke in vivid steps down to the sea. I walked out across the gray-beige ripples of cool sand, each slap of water on the shore reminding me of home beyond the blue-black void, reminding me of far too much . . .

Roberto waved and I moved down the beach.

"Why are you so sad?" he asked, his accent making the ordinary words warmer, caressive.

I turned, bent over to pull off my sandals, the *tanachniot* I had bought in Old Jaffa. We walked, and with only a few sentences from each of us, all the veils were lifted.

"We could be together," he said, pointing to some bushy-covered dunes down the beach. His accent, his swarthy sexiness, the moonlight made the line seem amazing. We headed in the direction of the two sand dunes that rose like a dull parenthesis waiting to be filled with meaning, information.

An army base lay some miles down the coast, and now the night was ground up by the roar of a jeep tearing through the sand and then fading, its radio crackling like gravel in a can.

On that trip in 1978, my first visit to Israel, I was barely skimming the surface of a country that was quite unreal to me, but deeply moving. It represented a path my parents hadn't taken. After liberation from their concentration camps, they lived in Belgium for several years, then emigrated to the U.S., while my mother's surviving brother, Wolf, had headed for Israel as soon as he could. Uncle Wolf and his family sent pictures and occasional letters to us in New York. All of them looked dark and mysterious, especially my gorgeous cousin Asher and his older sister Shoshanah. But Israel to me had always seemed a half-formed fantasy despite the reality of their jobs, their home, their military service.

Although I was overwhelmed now by being in a Jewish country, bathing in it, I had very little contact and conversation with Israelis besides my aunt, uncle, and cousin Asher—and that was usually about American or Israeli politics. With nothing but infant Hebrew (it was my eight years of French that helped me the few times I got lost), I was isolated on my little island, hoping to see the sails of an English speaker approaching to rescue me. One evening I was at a wedding surrounded by people who didn't or wouldn't speak English. I can't remember now how I got there, but I remember the chilling fear and isolation amid the excitement, the food, the dancing. I belonged—after all, Israel was my country if I wanted it to be—but I was unutterably foreign.

Back then, I had no real sense of myself as a gay man, so the idea of even trying to find lesbians and gay men in Israel never even occurred to me.

II

After talking with lesbian and gay American Jews who have lived and traveled extensively in Israel over the last fifteen years, I understand that I might not have found much gay life even *with* a knowledge of Hebrew. Back in the late seventies, gays in Israel were fairly invisible. "It was like the Chinese and Cubans saying, 'We don't have them here,'" American social worker Ron Ben-Ezra notes with a laugh. "Israelis thought it just didn't exist. They thought it was something European, or American."

Even today, with increased media attention in Israel to gay issues, gay life is far more low-key and closeted than in the U.S. At first glance, there may not be quite as many physical identifiers as there are in the U.S., since Israel is such a homogeneous society. Almost everyone has shared the experience of being in the military, for instance, and despite the various national origins or backgrounds, the majority of Israel's population is Jewish. San Diego restaurateur Alan Bilmes finds that, in Israel, "People tend to fall into place rather than do things differently." Most Israelis want to be mainstream, according to Ben-Ezra, who spent eight years in Israel.

But more significant than whether you can tell who's gay and who isn't, what you won't find in Israel is the vast panoply of bars, restaurants, clubs, saunas, bookstores, resorts, the gay music and entertainment—all the things American gays and lesbians take for granted, at least as a possibility. This absence of what we would consider a rich gay subculture is just one element of Israeli gay life, a life that may be hard for American gays to imagine, and one in which, paradoxically, disadvantages offer some promise.

Israel is a tiny country lacking in privacy. About the size of New Jersey or Connecticut, Israel is home to fewer than five million people. If you're gay or lesbian, you don't have the options that American gays do. It's not like growing up in the Midwest and moving to San Francisco or New York to come out, build a new life, and abandon everyone you knew who might not want to accept you. In Israel, that kind of separation from family and home just isn't possible. You can't re-create yourself like Gatsby. Many families are a lot tighter and more tolerant, "because they have to be," says Barbara Baum, a Pittsburgh Jewish community worker who spent fourteen years in Israel. "They can't make up stories about their children to pass off to neighbors, because the children are around or not far away."

Galia Goodman, an artist in Durham, North Carolina, spent about a year in Israel in the late eighties studying Hebrew and thinking about emigrating. She says that in Israel, "You can't escape the people who know the people you know. They're *everywhere*. You'll meet someone new who'll already have heard about you from a friend or a relative."

Baum said she found a remarkably "open" society. "The windows are always open," she recalls. "It's hard to have secrets."

Roger Kaplan recalls the day when he realized how very small a country Israel was. A Hebrew professor at Ohio State University, Kaplan has been to Israel more than half a dozen times since 1979. He recalls being on a hiking trip in the Golan Heights with his boyfriend, Uri. At least half an hour away from any town, they suddenly heard someone call "Hi!" Uri had run into his sister's ex-boyfriend from Tel Aviv.

While the ex-boyfriend did not assume that Roger and Uri were gay, Kaplan understood how hard it was to be gay in Israel. He also realized that if you're seen with someone who's known to be gay, there's "guilt by association." Most gays are so closeted you find that some don't use their full names when they sign letters in *Maga'im* (Contacts), one of the two gay magazines in Israel.

Feminist poet and historian Alice Young has spent time studying in Israel and working in the Israeli and Palestinian women's movement. Young observes that while Israeli lesbians may be aware of what they lack because the country is so small, Israel's size is "an advantage for an outsider." The lesbian community in Jerusalem is "tight and well organized," with regular meetings that are social and political.

Not only is Israel a small country, but "Israelis are nosy," says Bilmes, who travels to Israel at least once a year and has a wide network of friends there. "Israelis are blunt; they have no tact," says Baum. She had no intention of coming out there, but "they'll just ask you right out, or ask the person you buy eggs from. And he'll probably know!"

While more gays and lesbians are coming out, gay life to a large degree is still made up of cruising in public parks (for men), or meeting other lesbians and gays at private parties in people's homes. But even the privacy of someone's home is no protection against fear generated by being closeted. Goodman recalls, "I didn't meet anyone who was so open they felt comfortable with people being completely out." Goodman remembers women at parties walking into another room when someone showed up who was too politically active for them.

"They haven't grown up with positive gay role models," Kaplan observes. "So of course they're threatened by anyone who's out there." Ron Ben-Ezra was deeply involved in the growing politicization of Israeli gays, the move to decriminalize sodomy, and the legislation to end job discrimination against gays. As satisfying as that work was, he found that his political activity made it difficult to find and keep a lover.

Because Israel is so small and such a close-knit society, and because it's predominantly Jewish, there is tremendous cultural and social emphasis on family. "Noah's ark is real there," says Galia Goodman. "There's virtually no place for singles, gay or straight. Single women are perceived to be unhappy and there's tremendous pressure to be married. So gay friends tried setting me up with women, and straight friends who didn't know I was gay tried setting me up with men!"

Alan Bilmes recalls many supposedly straight married men cruising him on the street or trying to pick him up at parties. "It's no little land of virtue. And there's much more denial there than in the U.S." Goodman agrees. Women who are straight in Israel would most likely be lesbian in America, but they have husbands and children and are part of the community. "And if you come to Israel wondering if you're bisexual, there's so much emphasis on couples and marriage that you act out heterosexually." Goodman recalls conversations with other American Jewish lesbians who agreed that if for some reason they ended up stuck in Israel, they could see themselves getting married.

It is important to note that this emphasis on family life isn't identical with the right-wing Christian touting of family values so prevalent in the U.S. "Religion does shape attitudes in Israel," Kaplan finds, and Jerusalem may be fairly religious, but the country as a whole is not. Even though there are religious political parties that wield power in the government, homosexuality just isn't a significant issue for them. Those parties are far more interested in questions of religious education, stopping the desecration of burial sites, and the issue of territory. But there may also be an element of denial at work, Kaplan admits. Some Israelis might still want to insist that "Jews aren't homosexuals," so there's nothing to talk about.

Goodman is distressed by the impact of Israel's religious parties. "The Orthodox community has the country in a stranglehold. There's no separation of church and state, no civil marriage, which means there'll never be gay marriage." In more general terms, she sees the religious influence as undergirding the widespread assumption that everyone in Israel is straight. "It's irritating to feel so invisible there."

"For many Israelis," Bilmes says, "homosexuality is a non-issue. They may have strong personal opinions, but basically they see it as a question of privacy that's not their business." Barbara Baum thinks that Israeli bluntness is actually a good thing in some ways. "They'll blurt out things that people here [in the U.S.] only think. No one's playing games there or trying to be politically correct. You might come out to someone who says, 'You're disgusting,' then later asks you some questions about being gay, and comes to accept it more quickly because they're not *trying* so hard to be understanding."

Ron Ben-Ezra recalls that around eighty percent of the Israelis urged to sign petitions about ending employment-related discrimination agreed that it was not fair, irrespective of whether they thought homosexuality was moral or immoral. Most surprising to him was that it was not possible to predict who would sign a petition based on class, background, or age. "All those stereotypes went out the window for me. Even Orthodox Israelis signed."

But he and Alice Young both agree that the antigay stereotypes in Israel are identical with those in the U.S.: Gay men are seen as effeminate, recruiting, child molesters; lesbians as "mannish" and man-hating. Ben-Ezra has heard an interesting twist on the stereotypes about the causes of homosexuality. Apparently some in the Hasidic community believe that if a woman thinks lascivious thoughts while conceiving, her son will be a homosexual!

In some ways, the fact that homosexuality is not a burning political or social issue may work to the benefit of lesbians and gays in Israel. As Jews, they are very well integrated and that may be one reason homophobia does not seem as powerful and pervasive a social force as in the U.S. Galia Goodman says she never felt physically threatened there as a lesbian. Ben-Ezra not only felt safe enough there to be physically affectionate in public, but safer than in New York, though he notes the increasing incidence of gay bashing as Israeli society has become more violent. On the other hand, Alice Young notes a surge in domestic violence, and recalls how menaced she felt as a woman on her first trip to Israel in 1971. She was threatened by a soldier who followed her home from the beach. While she believes that it's still generally unsafe for women in a militarized society, she feels "totally safe" now with a solid base of lesbian friends and colleagues. But Barbara Baum says that straight and lesbian women face constant harassment in Israel.

Ben-Ezra, Young, and Baum have all been involved with recent political developments as Israeli lesbians and gays have become more public.

Ben-Ezra has seen a major revolution in gay visibility and awareness in the last ten years. A member of the Society for the

Protection of Personal Rights (SPPR), and its political arm, Otzma (Power), he has seen the group's board become increasingly feminist and activist in tone, where it was once primarily social in focus. Initially, it was hard to get media coverage for its activities, but recently gay people and gay issues are much more visible in the Israeli press. That is partly due to what Ben-Ezra calls "a new generation of reporters" who are more open. He remembers a story about gay cops in Tel Aviv being fired becoming a news sensation in 1991, with reporters "baying" for information from the SPPR. A recent Gay Pride-related press conference got what Ben-Ezra called "serious attention and intelligent press," and a gay film festival had sell-out crowds.

Other broader social changes have affected gay life in Israel, Ben-Ezra believes. Over the last ten years, Israelis have grown richer, have traveled more, and their increased exposure to European and American attitudes have made Israel more cosmopolitan. Anxieties about AIDS have also made Israeli society more aware, and sharpened the focus on gay concerns. Israel's HIV-positive rate is reported to be .2 percent per 1,000, but there's been a steady upsurge in HIV screening among all groups in the country's seven AIDS clinics, according to the *Detroit Jewish News*.

"Women in Black" is one of the first groups in Israel to urge the country's leaders to give up the West Bank and Gaza, using public demonstrations to raise consciousness. Alice Young notes that lesbians have played a major role in the group and in the Israeli women's movement in general. Young sees hope and excitement in the growing contacts developing between Israeli and Palestinian women. And her "uplifting" work with women makes her feel "hopeful and happy." Barbara Baum, also part of Women in Black, feels very positive about recent developments. "There really is a gay culture in Israel, and in Tel Aviv, gays almost seem to predominate."

Roger Kaplan is not so sanguine. Despite the changes, he detects a "strain of pessimism in Israeli gay men, who don't understand about achieving gay power, and even feel you have to look for a non-Israeli lover to be happy. It's a pre-Stonewall consciousness."

Israeli gays and lesbians have overcome some major legal obstacles that still face American gays, and Israel's Prime Minister Yitzhak Rabin, a former army chief of staff, says without equivocation that there is no reason to discriminate against gays in the military. Yet that discrimination continues, albeit inconsistently. Some people lose security clearance or don't get promoted as quickly as they might if they were straight, although Ron Ben-Ezra claims that it's widely known in Israel that much of military intelligence is gay.

Israelis leaving the country get more information about AIDS, which is still seen to be a foreign problem, than those already there. Tel Aviv now has a gay community center, but Bilmes sadly notes that it's underused. Yet over one hundred gays and lesbians met with ten Knesset members at the Knesset in February 1993 under the auspices of MK Yael Dayan, creating a media sensation.

Barbara Baum firmly believes that Israelis are becoming more tolerant and more aware. She cites as one example a class at Tel Aviv University's family counseling program: a required course in counseling gay couples. And because Israelis are more politically involved as a culture, there's hope for gays and lesbians as they become more open and political. Given how small Israel is, they're likely to see and feel the results of their efforts in ways American lesbians and gays cannot. The windows may be all that are wide open now, but the closet doors will surely follow.

III

So what happened with Roberto at the kibbutz? The sex was mostly exciting, but our few days together proved to be a disappointment. He was as deeply closeted as I was, so that it was impossible for us to talk about what we wanted from each other, or how we felt. At one midnight campfire on the beach, he freaked out when I reached for his hand in front of the other volunteers. I ended up fleeing the kibbutz just like I'd fled the U.S.

I'm not remotely like that now. The next time I go to Israel, it will be with my Jewish partner of ten years. Gersh and I are supporters of the SPPR and we donated money for Tel Aviv's gay community center. Friends have promised to put us in touch with gay men and lesbians there and we hope to explore gay life with as much passion as we'll explore the country itself. I want to show him Masada, and Old Jaffa, and walk on that kibbutz beach, admiring the lights of Haifa. Maybe there'll be a moon. . . .

Losing My Mother: Scenes from a Memoir

4

Losing My Mother: Scenes from a Memoir

~~Losing My Mother~~

Today, my mother is in ruins, the blurred outline of a person. Rigid, eyes vacant, leaning sideways in a wheelchair, almost bald, eyes rheumy, she has to be fed. It takes my father two hours to get the food inside her unavailing mouth.

My brother holds her nose to force her mouth open. His way, she's fed in half an hour, forty minutes, tops. My father can't do it like that.

Face collapsed, she recognizes no one, and is silent. It is a vast and horrible silence that she fell into after strange leave-takings. When the small strokes became more severe and crippling, when she had to be put—at seventy-three—on drugs to keep her from violence, she spoke with a foreign gentleness, like a kindly scientist explaining very complicated processes to children barely able to comprehend. Her voice so soft you had to lean in. What was she saying?

My father, shaking his head, but listening, listening, said, "Nonsense." And when I listened, I heard amid the Russian of her childhood what sounded like rhymes, wordplay of some kind.

"She's not saying anything," my father insisted.

I thought she was saying good-bye. Retreating first from English and even her everyday Yiddish with my father, back into her first language, what she spoke in St. Petersburg until 1919 or 1920, and in Vilno afterward, retreating into Russian baby talk.

The baby talk was almost the end. After that, the sentences dried up, halted, seeming to collide with an invisible barrier. Perhaps they were simply tired—the burden of carrying so much of a life, its beginning and its end, too much, too crippling.

Finally, silence, at first broken by an intermittent "yes" or "no" when my father asked if she recognized him, recognized anyone.

He was trying to lure her back into life through speech. The last full sentence I ever heard from her was "Oh, Alex, stop bothering me!"—in English—after he asked her three times if she knew who I was. He would not admit that she was vanishing; regarded the slightest change, the slightest flicker of attention as proof that she would get better.

Even now, when she's been institutionalized for more than a year, he can insist, "She knows everything I say." And he is excited and convinced that on some days she's better.

But then he had denied her illness, covered it, for at least a year before she was institutionalized.

I suspected something. When I called home, she sounded tired, distracted. He almost always answered the phone. Hoping in my own blind way for change in our relationship, I thought he might be wanting more closeness between us. I thought he *wanted* to talk to me.

He knew something was wrong with her, so he kept her from the phone.

And I was a little relieved not to talk to her. She had been an unstoppable talker all my life. Sometimes unbearable. Once I had a friend over and I was in agony to get my mother to shut up, to leave us alone, to stop being so engaging, so loquacious. I couldn't believe she was so out of touch with the moment. Painfully gauche.

Her charm was too desperate. She had a heavy laugh that strained her throat—an attempt at lightness that wasn't easy for her, and not just because of the chain smoking, and her dark, persistent cynicism.

She was witty, probing, inexhaustible, talking as if to fend off silence, questions, doubts, pain, examination. Politics, in endless ramifications. She devoured the *New York Times* and played it back even if you had read the identical article. She talked about literature too. Especially in her sixties when she went back to college, studied comparative literature and adored Derrida, Lacan, the most incomprehensible writers. How could you even call their work "writing"? It was mud thrown at a screen. Yet she dug through the mud, delighted, talking, talking, practically a straight-A student. For Mother's Day during the years she went to school I could send her—along with flowers—something like a volume of post-structuralist film criticism and she would be *delighted.*

Perhaps it was the same impulse that made her do puzzles, acrostics, and read mysteries: a drive to finish something, to make order and sense.

My brother says one day, "Don't come in and see her. It's too depressing."

I say I'll fly to New York if she's dying, but to me, she's already dead and even in my dreams, she has nothing left to say.

The deconstructionists my mother reveled in sometimes print words *sous rature* ("under erasure"): with lines running through them to highlight the inadequacy of those words. The word is there/the word is struck out. Living and dead at the same time.

This year, in Israel, my uncle tells me the barest details of a story about her years in concentration camps that I had never heard before. Once, in a Latvian camp, she felt someone was punished for something she inadvertently said, and she tried to kill herself.

A German doctor saved her life.

The Holocaust swallowed her family, her home, her youth. Silence now has swallowed her past.

My brother says another day, "Maybe if you came in, she'd recognize you."

There is no magic to bring her back to life, to words.

My mother is under erasure.

Stories . . .

My mother had survived.

She had a striped concentration camp dress. She had a wooden ring with a number on it, but I didn't know where she had worn either. She never told me. She told me too little/too much.

When I was young, when I was not so young, when I was a teenager and even in college, we sat in the L-shaped kitchen. A grim, ordinary Washington Heights Depression-era kitchen with a view of a gray side street out across a gated airshaft. We sat at the table that I saw years later in the window of a Los Angeles fifties kitsch shop: curving aluminum legs, ribbed aluminum sides topped by gray-patterned Formica, the poor man's marble. The table in L.A. was lit as if it were a Merovingian relic. But where was my mother to make it real?

We sat and drank coffee and talked about school and life and books and whatever. But there was always another presence there at the table in that quiet room: the haunted, haunting past. The past that emerged in stories, or bits of stories. Maybe just flashes. These stories slipped into my life, like an unseen cat that suddenly springs to slash your hand.

They didn't happen to me, but they're mine, now, or at least what I can remember of them. And so they live inside me, making me—sometimes—afraid of crowds. The panic I have felt in a football stadium after a game as hordes surge down the ramps, and I am swept along, powerless to pull myself away or out, powerless to stop. Feeling I want to scream so they'll let me go. Flashes.

— *"In ghetto"* (those words were in Yiddish), "we ground up glass and wrapped it with a little food to put in the rat holes, then stuffed the holes with whatever we could find." I think I was supposed to admire her cleverness. The resourceful Jews trapped by the Nazis, taking care of themselves. All I could think of was the rats, coming through the walls, my walls.

— "A Polish woman said to me, You can always tell a Jew. They have such sad eyes."

— "When they liquidated the ghetto, Polish women spit on us as we were marched out."

But here I have to stop. How old was I when those words became not just part of my vocabulary, but part of my life? Liquidated. Ghetto. This is not the imagination of disaster, this *is* disaster. I will never not know these words or foggy images. I will never escape.

— "They shaved our heads." Here, she breaks off, and the words float in my memory like a ragged cloud, with only empty sky around it. She rarely said even those four words together. But years later, I think they hide behind a different pain. When my mother starts losing her hair, the hair that was luxuriant, alive— before the War, and even after for some years. She suffers new defeats. In all of New York, she can't find a wig that looks good. But then, what wig can hide the losses no one sees? She tries some vitamins, and wisps of hair grow back, but cannot hide her higher brow. I suggest a different man to cut and style and dye her hair, but she erupts in tears, pleading to be let alone: "There is no hair there!"

It's hopeless is what she means, but I press and press, wanting her to hope, just a little, just about her hair, her looks, something. She was so beautiful once, and now she's given up. Or so it seems to me, a boy who hasn't lived in hell.

Gas

I came to dread the ringing of the phone. Because of times like this—times before I knew how sick my mother was:

Casually, my brother Sam tells me, "Mom isn't going out as much. She has gas."

This is not a conversation I want to have. Yet I cannot help asking, "Gas? Why? What's wrong?"

"It's her ulcer medication, I think."

"Can't they give her something for the gas?" But even I know that she probably hasn't mentioned it to her doctor. Embarrassment. "And what about shopping?"

"Dad does it."

I don't know what to say. I'm appalled to talk about my mother's gas. Partly, it's the word itself. Farting is a different word, a different world—farting is funny, farting is Chaucer. And for me, a writer, it's distance. The Age of Farts: a literary epoch in which farting is a part of life, something you can write about with joy.

But gas is something else. Gas is death. It has been a dirty word for me as long as I can remember. Gas killed my mother's mother, and countless other Jews.

Desperate to quell the moles creating their condos in my gorgeous backyard, I hesitantly buy gas shaped like sticks of dynamite. Poison pellets haven't worked, and the thought of steel and crushing traps disgusts me. Gas is all that's left.

I'm in the gardening aisle of a local supermart. Boxes and bottles promising death to pests face bottles and boxes trumpeting growth and blooms. I lurk like someone in an adult bookstore afraid of being recognized. I make my shoddy purchase and tell no one how ashamed I am to gas even unseen life. But I feel like a murderer anyway. And then, I'm slightly relieved, because the gas has no effect except to drive *me* from the yard.

My mother's gas. No end to cruelty. The ghetto, the starvation, the camps. And now my mother once again is trapped. By gas. Like Mrs. Mendelssohn, my piano teacher for eight years. Rose Mendelssohn, a Russian Jew. Frail, slim, dithering, in her seventies, one day at our lesson, she has gas. Shocked, sixteen or so, I sit there as she plays some frantic chords to drown the crescendo of stuttering from inside herself. As if it weren't there. Banging out those chords. Crescendo. Hiss. She says nothing. I say nothing. But soon I understand that this is why her lessons have dried up. I know this is why her apartment in our building has a strange metallic smell.

It isn't long before she stops her lessons, or they stop her, and I have no more interest in the piano anyway. It isn't long before she's locked inside her apartment and the super's wife stands outside the black steel-clad door, calling, "Rosie, Rosie, come out." Like a children's game. Finally, the woman phones one of Mrs. Mendelssohn's daughters. They take her "away."

All this happens offstage. I hear it from my mother, who sneers at Mrs. Mendelssohn's rich children. Children off in some suburb, who rarely descend from their heights to our deteriorating Washington Heights, children who have abandoned their mother (so my mother says). Abandoned her to a stale apartment where she doesn't wash or clean or eat, but broods or drifts, a gentle wraith.

"I don't want to end up like that," my mother says. Over and over. This is her greatest fear, greater than expecting cancer, which she does whenever she is weak or ill.

My mother's aunt also wound up "like that," sliding into oblivion, knowing nothing in her eighties but regrets and accusations.

I remember reading of the camps, of gas, of Nazi gas. And more: the Jews, their guts betrayed by lack of food, betraying. Everything stripped away, including dignity. Especially dignity.

On some slave labor crew digging, hauling rocks, my mother says a man called out "Hey you!" to a German Jew, who reared up. "I am Herr Doktor Professor Schmidt—not 'hey you!'"

"You're just a stinking Jew like all the rest of us," is the reply. And yes, they stink. No wonder my mother was always fastidious, talked and nagged at home about "hygiene."

How has she come to this? Once elegant, battered now by time, bursting inside, drawing inward from the world. It mortifies me to think of her reduced to helplessness.

And, most horribly, I recall the last time I was home, how she didn't know I was awake—I think—and there was a thunderclap of gas beyond belief when she awoke and made her bed.

I tell none of this to Sam.

Smoking

"Tiny white spots on the brain," my father repeats.

I have asked him what the doctor said, what the MRI showed, what it all means, what the name is, hoping to find power in a word or words. He can't remember.

I ask again. Exasperated, my father says, "What do I know what it's called? It's tiny white spots on the brain—I saw the picture."

"But that's not the name of an illness—that's . . ."

Well, what is it?

Like those brutal black and white photos of bombed Iraq. I see the territory of her brain laid waste. Not so long before, I had been haunted by air raid sirens on the nightly news—in Israel, Saudi Arabia, and Iraq. I imagined the terror of waiting for bombs to strike, the noise, the concussion, the stench, the utter powerlessness. It was impossible for me to hear the sirens and not picture my mother and her parents trapped at a funeral in a hurricane of German bombs in 1941, or my father—a slave laborer for the Hungarian army—digging trenches under constant bombardment by the Soviets.

How is there so much violence in her brain?

I'm driving from LaGuardia airport with my father to see why my mother is locking herself out of the apartment, losing her keys, waiting for him downstairs hours before he's due to come home.

"Mom called me to ask what every four hours means," my brother has said. "For one of her prescriptions." This prompted my flight from Michigan. My alarm turns to despair when my father and I misconnect at the airport and we look for each other for half an hour. I call their home and my mother drowsily repeats, "He went to the airport to pick up the man who is arriving."

She doesn't know who I am right now, she's confused, can't take a message, can't follow what I try to tell her.

It's worse than I thought. A series of small strokes has ripped apart the woman she was. Now my father keeps asking, "You think it's bad?" after telling me each new horror in the car, after lamenting, "The poor girl—the poor girl. How can this happen to her?"

I want to scream at him. I want to make him drive like the young man he is not, instead of letting his right foot ease on and off the gas pedal as if he sat at a sewing machine. I want to flee whatever is ahead.

"Such a sickness, it never was in my family," my father says.

"Strokes can be caused by smoking. It's probably all the smoking," I say. "That's not hereditary. Two packs a day—"

"No. Mother never smoked like that."

"Two packs a day!"

Furious, he denies it. But I know two is close to the truth. I used to run out and buy her Larks for her. We wrangle. But it must be true.

Like dogs growling over a blanket tugged tight between them, we go back and forth about her smoking. I begin to wonder if he's right.

The next day I relay this conversation to my brother, who smiles as if my father's denial of reality is nothing new.

"But she did smoke a lot, didn't she?" I'm begging to be believed.

"All the time," Sam says, though that's no longer our concern.

Just to be sure, that weekend I call my oldest friend to check. Thankfully she says, "Lev, I never saw your mother *without* a cigarette. She was a chain smoker. Really."

But why did I badger my father? What difference did it make what caused the nightmare in her brain, the cave-in, the collapse? Why can't we grieve together?

I am blaming him, my mother, me.

The bombs have hit us all and left us dazed amid the smoking ruins.

Names

Names are nothing constant in a life. My father's name is Alex now, but never was for years. He was born as Shlomo. Solomon. A name with history and grandeur (unlike the nickname Shloimy), connected to the Jewish past. But in a time when Nazis and their friends destroyed the Jewish present, past, and future, burning people, books, and towns, his name was lost.

Captured by Hungarians, he became Szandor. Like a flooded valley where the towns lie ghostly underneath the brand new lake, he was Shloimy still. And underneath there was more. He was descended from the Temple priests, a Levi, and then so was I.

But he was nothing much to the Hungarians. He never was a man, he's just a Jew.

They used him as a tool, dragged him with the other slaves on their way to fight the Soviets. He dug trenches in the winter blasts, his shovel striking sparks on frozen ground.

But he survived. Survived the guard who threw a hand grenade at him but killed his friend. My father sports the shrapnel in his legs—a lasting gift. His friend's head disappeared in chunks.

And he survived his flight, his hiding with a priest who taught him Latin prayers to masquerade. Recounting this, he cried.

Stolen name and stolen faith. Another flight and he was captured, finally, in Budapest or Prague (which one, which one?), and shipped to Bergen-Belsen, where a German pointed a gun at his head and asked his name. He didn't fire, smiling: They had the same last name.

I learned all this in his isolated moments of recall. He would start speaking as if overcome, a medium in touch with worlds beyond, and questions would have stopped the flow, so I said nothing, just brought him schnapps to down.

Somewhere in these scraps of narrative I learned he faced an execution once, or did my mother tell me that? Faced a firing squad, but British bombers overhead delayed his death.

And I learned he fought guerrilla war, sharpshooting from some hills. I only knew this when he read a movie sign from blocks away, amazing me. "That's nothing. I could shoot a Nazi from much farther away."

In his accent *farther* sounded like *fodder*. Which he was.

And afterwards, in postwar time, marooned in Brussels, Szandor made a Belgian Alexandre, shortened on his Brussels documents to Aleks.

My mother's name also suffered transformation. Born in Petrograd, she was Lia Helena. Lia disappeared in Poland, I don't know why, and living with my father for five years in Brussels once they were free, her name was Hélène.

But Americans couldn't stand the foreignness in 1950, and it was bleached away to dowdy Helen, stripped of euphony and grace.

There was a deeper loss. My father's family name, Steinberg, was not his own, or not for long. It was the imposition of an eighteenth-century Austrian law that Jews should have real (German) names. "Stein" means stone and "berg" means mountain—an empty, brutish German name.

No wonder Sam, my brother, wants to change his name. Born in Brussels, he is only Sam, there's no trace of French about him.

He'd like to be "Alain," at least to add it onto Sam—a middle name where he has none.

"Why not?" I say, but something holds him back.

Not me. Twice, I've named myself. Once to wrestle free, to be myself. I chose my uncle's name, the one who died at Stalingrad. And Lev meant many things. Heart in Hebrew. Lion in Yiddish. Two pieces of my life.

And then again, five years along, I dropped my father's name and chose one that means "God will heal" to mark my new connection to my faith.

I escaped the German branding iron, decolonized myself.

Came down from my father's mountain, as, I think, my brother can't or won't.

Lines

It wasn't a bedtime story. Nothing to make me sleep. It was a nightmare. My mother in one line, her mother in the other. The line going to the right: to gas, to death, to flames.

Is it any wonder my mother was obsessed for years with asking if the stove is off? Leaving the apartment, driving off, she'll say, "Alex? Did I turn off the stove?" What is her vision? Gas and flames ripping apart the life she has, the life she rescued from the past?

I do it, too. Older now, perhaps as old as she was when I first noticed her concern. I ask Gersh, Did you check the stove? Sometimes he laughs; sometimes I dread that passenger inside, that memory of her in fear.

It's an electric stove, but still I can see myself driving back to find our home a black and ugly pile, destroyed. The quiet tree-lined street scarred by smoke and stink. My secret terrors. Like hearing noises late at night and imagining a murderer, a gun or many knives. I know from my own parents' past that nothing is ever safe. Most of the time, it is knowledge I suppress.

Those fatal lines. Was that the same scene, the same camp where an elegant woman opened a casket of jewels for the Nazi officer in charge to beg for freedom, or at least for life? You can imagine what she got, my mother adds, and I don't ask.

Torn apart. From home, from friends, from family, from life. I worry when Gersh is late, or doesn't call when he said he would. I fear an accident, his death.

My brother says he heard a different story about lines. My mother told him something else. That her mother understood the meaning of the lines at once, shoved my mother across to life, to hope, despite her cries. Someone beat them both and that was all. My mother lived. Knowing she was saved by her own mother's hands.

Who could live with such a scene? And yet she did. Maybe that's the scene that came back when my mother's brain caught fire, when she attacked my brother, my father too, threw plants across the room, and shouted out in German.

I couldn't bear to ask for more, to ask what words returned to her, what pain. Knowing they were German was bad enough. I have rarely heard her speak that poisoned tongue.

I wonder why she told us different versions of the truth. Was there some lesson we should learn? Did Sam know more because he's older, because he heard it closer to the past? As she grew older, was that crucial shove too much to think about, repeat?

Who would *I* save knowing that it meant my life?

Castles

Books made great walls. Before I learned how to read, I would drag my brother's hardback books from the three-shelved beige bookcase at one end of our large open room, scooch down by the big cardboard box full of toys, and proceed to build a "castle." Cross-legged and happy on the gray-, red-, and black-flecked linoleum, chattering to myself, I'd stand the books on end, creating square keeps with massive double doors that could either slide or swing open. I wasn't concerned with scale, except to try to make the books fairly even in height. The smooth, shiny covers, usually monochrome, made the walls seem resolute and unscalable.

The big fat books were the most satisfying, like one about bees and ants, with a glossy maroon cover.

Plastic figures of all kinds—animals, men, it didn't matter—would march along the tops as if behind thick battlements, taunting their enemies, protecting themselves, surveying their domain.

These were not the elegant, pennoned castles of my cutout books, where each brick looked as real as the artist could make it. And though I could use the cutout knights on my book battlements, they bent or tore and were only two-dimensional, while my own castles had three dimensions, if not more.

My book castles didn't have the solidity and grace of the ones I could make using the light brown blocks we kept in a cloth bag, blocks that clattered against each other when I lifted the bag from my toy box. There were some triangles and arches among the blocks, and along with the squares and rectangles, I could use these to simulate towers and doorways in a castle that wasn't likely to tip over, as the books might. But the neutral-colored blocks weren't as exciting, unless I mixed them up in some way with the books.

The books were always more satisfying. The walls higher and thicker, guarding the secrets inside.

I wanted to be inside those walls, protected, safe.

There was too much anger outside those walls, too much shouting and pain.

I didn't know then that my parents had survived concentration camps, but I knew they had come from somewhere else, from

Europe—a land of castles and knights in my imagining—and had somehow been imprisoned.

But they were still in prison.

And I picked up this fear, I played with it. Coming home from school, I'd imagine our building besieged. Some enemy was swarming in from the street. I held them off at the buzzer door, then from behind a barricade in the hall, always falling back, but always resilient. It was a mental tic, a game, a spell. Practicing destruction.

I used colored clays to build castles in the bathroom sink, whose walls I breached to see the water flow, and drown whatever was inside.

It was an easy game to play. I lived in a castle. Our building was on one of the many hills of Washington Heights. The dark wide lobby was gloomy, and picturesque with its sconces, carved tables, deep window embrasures, and touches of marble. Coming home, walking in off a fairly treeless stretch of Broadway, was like entering another era.

Our apartment was on the eighth floor, and one of the windows in the bedroom I shared with Sam was a double window with a glittering view of upper Manhattan, the Hudson River, the tree-thick Palisades, the sturdy, graceful George Washington Bridge, and the hilly, mysterious overgrown cemetery of downtown's Trinity Church. It was like being in a tower.

There were castles all around me. The local library, off 145th Street, near the Gothic-looking elementary school.

My notebooks were full of towers, castles. I liked the idea of being far away and enclosed.

The first thing I remember painting in school was a tower on a hill. The easel stood at the back of class, and I didn't have much time there. The paints ran. When I did any art project, the clumsiness of my hands undid me.

I was safer with my books.

Writing Something Real

5

Writing Something Real

All through college, my creative writing teacher kept predicting that I would be published someday, even win prizes, but not until I wrote something "real." I didn't know what she meant at the time, although I can see it now. I was writing comic sketches about working-class couples, and what I thought of as high English farce. I even attempted a gothic romance about a girl locked in a tower by her father who played Beethoven in the gloomy parlor below, while she lamented her fate and wrote tearful sonnets. I'd read one too many Victoria Holt novels, I guess.

My writing was as far away from myself as possible, and by that I mean, as far away from my world, my own observations, my own truest knowledge. It was secondhand, drawn from other people's books.

Yet it was two classic novels I read in my senior year that first opened me up to my own depths, connected me to myself in such a way that I could never quite return to falseness and hiding—at least in my writing. Edith Wharton's *The House of Mirth* and Henry James's *The Portrait of a Lady* had a lasting impact on me by forcing me to begin confronting my own demons: the fear of being gay, and my unwillingness to claim a positive Jewish identity.

What was in these two books that kept me reading into the middle of the night, breathless, transfixed, aware of myself as utterly changed? Wharton's masterpiece is the story of a woman destroyed by a society that offers her one choice alone: marriage. There is no other way for Lily Bart to live the life she has been trained to expect as rightfully hers because she is beautiful, graceful, and gifted with impeccable taste. Perhaps the most crushing moment in the book takes place on the Riviera, when Lily is publicly and unmistakably branded as an adulteress. Soon after, she discovers that she is virtually disinherited by the aunt who has not too generously taken care of her since her parents' death, in part because of that scene. Twin humiliations: two moments in which Lily Bart is alone, stared at, the object of scorn and pity, and irrevocably cast out. Life's hopes and possibilities continually elude and defeat Lily.

James's heroine, Isabel Archer, a free-spirited, optimistic, and challenging woman, finds that a huge inheritance leads her into a blind alley. In the novel's most poignant chapter, Isabel understands that the man she married, hoping to give herself a wider view of life, is really the exact opposite of what she expected. He is petty, mean, and shallow. She feels hopeless and trapped; her imagined home of free expression and love openly given and received is really "the house of dumbness, the house of deafness, the house of suffocation."

That was the emotional house that I lived in. Although I had known I was attracted to men from first grade on, I had never allowed myself to carry this attraction forward into anything more than furtive hugs and soppy poetry. Instead, I dated women, compelled by the dictates of a society that even in liberated 1970s New York hated homosexuals. I could not face the possibility of being scorned and cast out as Lily Bart had been.

I am a first-generation American. My first language was Yiddish, not English.

When I started writing fiction in earnest in high school and college, it expressed my desire to erase my difference, to flee into another reality, any reality. My writing was profoundly un-Jewish, it said nothing about the Holocaust, and ignored sexual conflict.

I was afraid of outrage and retribution both from non-Jews for being Jewish and from Jews for being gay. I had seen and studied the incredible uproar in the Jewish community generated by Philip Roth's *Portnoy's Complaint,* which was published as I entered adolescence (you can imagine what that did to my thinking about sex). This book terrified me. Roth wrote that what made the book so infamous is that no one expects a Jew to go crazy in public. Not Jews, and especially not non-Jews, who, as Portnoy says, "own the world and know absolutely nothing about human boundaries."

This was not mere rhetoric to me, this was *real.* My parents had seen their neighbors in Poland and Czechoslovakia eliminate human boundaries. And so I was not only afraid of betraying *them,* but also of exposing myself to potentially hostile non-Jewish eyes. No wonder my fiction was full of disguises. It read like a series of desperate flares sent up for help.

My creative writing teacher in college understood those flares, and she was the first person I came out to.

I did it on the phone one evening, because I figured if it went badly I could always hang up.

"Kris," I said. "I have something to tell you."

"Do a need a drink to hear this?" I didn't catch the irony in her reply, just the warmth.

"Yes—a big one."

"Wait a minute—hold on—don't hang up!" I heard a cabinet door open, the clink of bottles, glassware, ice.

"I'm back."

Whispering now, unable to hang up, driven by the urge to tell someone and captured by the momentum of release, I said, "I have these feelings—" I couldn't go further, but she did, nonchalantly.

"Feelings about men?"

Her insight and lack of surprise made me laugh. And later I found out that two other students in the same class had come out to her, not long before. Also on the phone. But her ease wasn't mere practice or pedagogy, it was the natural expression of a nurturing wise woman whose gift was seeing potential in her students— potential of many kinds. I registered for every class she taught.

In her novel classes, I read authors that took me deeper into myself: Samuel Butler, Dreiser, James, Fitzgerald, George Eliot, Edith Wharton. In her writing workshops, she kept up the pressure on me to write something, anything, that was real. Yes, my medieval fantasies were amusing, but I was floating on the surface of the story. Every story. My own stories.

My senior-year conflicts about whether I should marry a non-Jewish girl, in combination with reading Wharton and James, finally propelled me into writing that was unmistakably more real, writing that dealt with characters' feelings as facts and not fantasies, writing that traveled into uncertainties of the heart and not mere plot complications, writing that didn't constantly pat itself on the back for being so clever. This new depth was unexpectedly aided by the theater courses I was taking. Not because I learned about myself in rehearsal and onstage, but because I had never before felt so tantalized and so completely an outsider. Never truly their equal or even their colleague, I was moved to write and observe the other students in this self-dramatizing, cliquish, mean-spirited department. I was suddenly a budding anthropologist, recording details of an alien world.

In my graduate writing program a year later, I was drawn on to new discoveries, not all of them pleasant. I learned that the need for a man had been so stifled in me by internalized homophobia, by my own shame, that I could not only accept an unsatisfactory and even demeaning relationship, but glory in it as if living an opera. Surely I *deserved* to feel tormented? But I also learned the joy of being with other writers, of taking myself seriously, and of being published in *Redbook* at twenty-four.

In Amherst, for the first time in my life I gave way completely to the admission that I wanted another man. This wasn't a fantasy, this was the provocative presence of someone in my dorm. I said the words—I wrote it down in my journal. He had dropped by my room one night to chat—a large broad Viking of a man, easygoing, sensuous, relaxed. That week, I had been reading two novels of obsession: Susan Hill's eerie *The Bird of Night* and *Wuthering Heights;* I was primed for an explosion of *some* kind. While Fred and I talked, suddenly I *saw* him with complete clarity at the same time that I knew I wanted him, desperately, with such force that the frenzy of my pulse made me wonder why every item in the room didn't burst apart.

The revelation devastated me afterwards—I could feel a tremendous shift inside, and knew I was in the middle of a crisis in which the decision seemed to be: Stop writing and hide, or keep writing and open up. To write at all, to write honestly, was to stir up everything inside of me that was painful and unresolved.

I had written a paragraph describing a character's father and knew it was the entrance into a story I had to tell—and was afraid to tell. After I called Kris and read it to her on the phone, she urged me to keep writing, in fact, made me agree to write a section, call her and read it to her, write another, call her—and so on until it was done a day and a half later. I was terrified—I was alive.

It was a story about the son of Holocaust survivors who felt alienated by his parents' past, and crushed by it. Writing that story, staying open, was a choice.

My writing workshop hated the story, and so did the professor.

It's very satisfying to report that two weeks later, Martha Foley, editor of *The Best American Short Stories,* awarded it the Harvey Swados Prize. A year later, it was published in *Redbook,* which then had 4.5 million readers. I was being taken seriously as a writer, I was making money on my work.

But publishing in *Redbook* led me into typical New York blindness. Starting there, winning a prize—weren't those natural first steps of an easy ascent to cash and fame?

For five or six years after that, every story I sent to national magazines and even the major literary quarterlies was rejected. Opening the mailbox I felt assaulted by the manila envelopes— sometimes five in a day—defeated, crushed. It was my own misjudgment; I thought that everything I wrote was as good as my first publication. I thought the only place worth publishing was in a magazine like *Redbook*, or better. In Michigan, I could slowly cut loose of those expectations and ask simple questions: What did I have to say in my writing? Who was my audience?

A story I wrote in one evening was the first to break the drought. It was accepted immediately by a Jewish magazine, and my stories began to appear in a widening range of Jewish publications. I became something of a Jewish celebrity in East Lansing (which I can imagine my father dismissing as a *knappeh metziah*— no big deal).

But feeling restored as a writer, hopeful again, and finally connected as a Jew, I was only halfway there. It wasn't until I fell in love with my partner, Gersh—who is Jewish—that I was able to begin bridging the two worlds. It was loving him and being loved (feeling safe) that gave me the courage to write my first gay *and* Jewish short story—an early version of the title piece of my collection *Dancing on Tisha B'Av*. And when it was included in a national anthology of gay fiction a few years after being published in an obscure Jewish magazine, I suddenly had a new audience developing. Ultimately what brought me the most attention as a writer was adding another circle of readers by stepping out into a gay audience, but unmistakably as a Jew.

The refusal to accept silence and marginalization, the impor-

tance of speaking for ourselves, of telling stories, have become re-
curring themes of my fiction. My writing is deeply Jewish not just
in subject matter, but in its sense of the urgency to break every con-
stricting silence. Jews have always been enjoined to tell their stories:
The Book of Amos says, "Tell your children of it." But telling our
stories does more than keep memory alive, it creates something
new. It builds bridges between communities, helps people find
pride in their identity, and breaks the hold of silence.

The epigraph for *Dancing on Tisha B'Av* is from Don DeLillo's
brilliant novel *Players:* "To speak it in words is to see the possibilities emerge." Some of the possibilities I hope will emerge from my
fiction are greater understanding among non-Jews of the continuing impact of the Holocaust. I hope that Jews and non-Jews will
appreciate the parallels between society's oppression of gays and
anti-Semitism. I hope straight Jews will come to see the place of
gay and lesbian Jews in American Judaism. And for lesbian and gay
Jews in particular, I want my fiction to say what Jews say after
someone has had an honor during a Torah service, *yasher koach*—
may your strength be multiplied.

Letter from Israel, II

6

Letter from Israel, II

I once asked a friend who spent lots of time in Israel what gay life was like there and he ruefully said, "They have a pre-Stonewall consciousness."

But that was before May 30, 1994, when four screaming right-wing demonstrators interrupted a wreath-laying ceremony by gays and lesbians at Yad Vashem, Israel's Holocaust memorial and museum in Jerusalem. The resulting melee made news worldwide and thrust Israeli gays and lesbians to center stage in the Israeli media in a way they never expected (and some regret).

I was in Israel for two weeks with my partner, Gersh. We had started the day of the Yad Vashem ceremony in Jerusalem and visited the Western Wall on the first of four days of intensive touring around Israel before the conference. Our travels would also involve spending lots of time with Israeli gays.

The ceremony was the first and most solemn event of a week leading up to an Israeli and European conference of gay and lesbian Jews at Givat Haviva, a kibbutzlike conference center an hour or so north of Tel Aviv. Several days before May 30, a group of American rabbis had taken an ad in the *Jerusalem Post* decrying the planned ceremony and talking about gays in the blood-and-thunder language American gays are used to hearing from the religious right. The stage was thus set for some kind of confrontation at a spot that is sacred in many ways to Israelis and Jews everywhere. Foreign leaders visiting Israel invariably lay wreaths in Yad Vashem's Hall of Remembrance at the eternal flame, and various Jewish groups often do the same. This, however, was the first time that such an event was sponsored by Israel's gay and lesbian civil rights group, the Society for the Protection of Personal Rights (SPPR).

On May 30, one hundred and fifty Israeli, European, and American gay Jews waited to say prayers in memory of gay and lesbian Jews who died in the Holocaust. Many were children of Holocaust survivors. We stood along the raised broad platforms forming two sides of the Hall of Remembrance, whose black granite floor bears the names of concentration camps that are seared into my family's history, and into the memory of the Jewish people—names like Majdanek, Bergen-Belsen, Auschwitz, Stutthof.

The short ceremony started with singing of the Song of the Vilno Ghetto Partisans and chanting of prayers, but it was almost immediately interrupted by a hysterical demonstrator who was later identified as a member of Israel's banned right-wing Kach party. He shrieked, tore his hair, and rolled on the ground, calling us "evil," saying we were "full of shit" and worse, accusing us of blasphemy, of desecrating the site. This same man claimed that his father had been murdered (some news stories said raped) by a homosexual Nazi camp guard.

The ceremony went on in the midst of chaos, as eager cameramen scurried like cockroaches after this man—and then another, and then two more—while Yad Vashem attendants and police tried to subdue and eject them.

Gersh and I were paralyzed. I wondered if this was what it was like during World War II in Europe—that is, seeing something so unbelievable that you were utterly unable to respond or know how to respond. Should I leave? Should I leap down from the platform onto the floor to make the demonstrators stop? I was amazed at the hatred I suddenly felt, wishing I could silence those monsters of intolerance.

The ceremony went on—even after someone snatched pages from the hand of the chanting gay rabbi. Some people shouted the words of the Kaddish (prayer for the dead) at the demonstrators to drown them out. Then we all locked arms and sung the poet and partisan Hannah Senesch's plangent and moving hymn "Eli, Eli." That was met by howling contempt: A demonstrator shouted that we were defiling her memory and her words because we were gay.

In half an hour, the ceremony and the uproar were over—or so I thought.

News coverage in the U.S. and even radio reports focused on the shouting and the apparent violence at Yad Vashem, but it missed the aftermath in Israel's media, which we were able to follow in detail along with our Israeli friends. Gays fared badly on Israeli TV, where the rhetoric on talk shows *starts* with the incendiary. But many Israeli newspapers strongly condemned the demonstrators' outrageous and ugly behavior. The speaker of the Knesset (who is a Holocaust survivor) accused them of "fascist" tactics in trying to silence their opponents, and said that if some of these protestors were survivors themselves, they had learned nothing from their ordeal.

Most inspiring was the reaction of fiery Knesset member Yael Dayan, who made it very clear that this attack on gays was linked to other hatreds: of Arabs, of secular Jews, of women. Dayan wrote in the *Jerusalem Post* that "anyone who believed in [Israel's] future as an egalitarian, democratic, humane society, one which accepts those who are different and supports their rights as a minority, ought to wear a pink triangle, next to the yellow star and blue-and-white."

Dayan was also the keynote speaker at the SPPR-sponsored conference which started four days after the Yad Vashem ceremony, and she received a standing ovation there before she spoke a word. At Givat Haviva, Dayan's empathy and anger were unswerving. Speaking to an audience of nearly three hundred Israeli, European, and North and South American Jewish gays and lesbians, she made it very clear that those fanatics in Israel who hated gays, objected to peace, and also objected to human rights — these people suffered "an inability to understand or accept the Other." Dayan said to us, "Your hurt is my outrage; your tears give me voice and strength." Gersh and I felt empowered and uplifted, wishing that there were more American politicians who could speak out for gays so unambiguously.

Reactions to the Yad Vashem incident among Israeli gays were very mixed. Some were elated at their sudden high visibility and the appearance in print of allies. Others, like Israel's premier gay poet, Ilan Schoenfeld, were stunned by the negative press. Schoenfeld was in an unrivaled position to chart these reactions because he was the SPPR's publicist for the conference. "My fax and my phone didn't stop ringing for days," he told us over lunch at Cafe Nordau, Tel Aviv's charming and very popular gay restaurant. He was afraid that the hostility aroused by the fracas at Yad Vashem would backfire on Israel's gays.

Yet many of the gays and lesbians I spoke to felt inspired by facing their critics, which is somewhat new, because gays in Israel are very closeted.

I saw how intimate (and intrusive) Israel could be when our tour visited Masada the day after the Yad Vashem incident. In the jammed cable car coming back down from the mountain palace-fortress built by King Herod, a woman asked our tour guide (who was also gay) if we were "the group" that had been at Yad Vashem (was it because some of us were enjoying being shoved together?). Our guide said yes, and the two of them fell into an increasingly fiery discussion in Hebrew in which she — herself a tour guide — denounced us for upsetting Israel's three hundred thousand Holocaust survivors. She was also worried about who would get married if there were too many gays and lesbians, and said she hoped none of her children were gay.

One of the highlights of our wonderful two-week trip was attending the opening of a used bookstore-coffee shop in Jerusalem's historic and very beautiful Nahalat Shiva district, the first independent Jewish settlement outside the old city walls, established in the mid-nineteenth century. With a pedestrian mall, gorgeous stone buildings, and lively restaurants, it's the very image of a confident, economically powerful Israel. David Erlich, the store's owner, is a young Israeli gay writer.

Israel's Nobel prize-winning poet Yehuda Amichai read that evening, and it seemed that hundreds of people were in and out all night, many of them friends of ours from the conference. At one point, someone took Gersh up to the front of the store. "See those two shelves in that bookcase? That's the first gay section in any bookstore in Israel." Many people told me that they went to London or Amsterdam to buy gay and lesbian books. The paucity of gay literature may explain the success of one of David Leavitt's books when it was translated into Hebrew.

"It's very hard to be a gay writer here," Schoenfeld told us, as he described the pressure from publishers to tone down the gay content of his work, and the various projects and anthologies he'd like to do if he only had the time and the access. Schoenfeld talked movingly about the possibility of starting a small gay press, but it was clearly one of many dreams, especially because Schoenfeld's publicity work takes so much of his time.

As I did my reading at Givat Haviva during the SPPR-sponsored conference, I was keenly aware that there was no gay *Israeli* poet or fiction writer on the program. After the reading, an Israeli man came up to tell me that his fiction was becoming more homoerotic, but he felt stymied about where to publish it. There wasn't much specific help I could offer.

When I told a gay writer friend I was going to be reading in

Israel, he said, "The homophobia must be terrible there." The extremely photogenic outbursts at Yad Vashem will no doubt confirm stereotypic views of Israeli society as deeply antigay, but the truth is much more complex, as I've described in my first "Letter from Israel" (chapter 3).

And despite the theatricality and publicity of the outbursts at Yad Vashem, it's hard to believe that antigay rhetoric will ever become a driving force in Israel's political scene, as it is in the U.S. An Israeli interviewer trying to get me and Gersh on a national radio show to talk about what happened at Yad Vashem wasn't concerned when our schedules didn't work out: "It's a big story now, but not for long."

Yet many of the Israelis discussing the incident at Tel Aviv's glossy new gay community center (which has a remarkably rich library of English-language gay titles) seemed to agree that "something like this had to happen." Gays and lesbians in Israel had to see the depth of the hatred in at least part of Israel's populace, had to see the worst facing them. "We're not babies anymore," I heard from several gay Israelis. More defiantly, more proudly, many said with a sense of discovery, "This is our Stonewall."

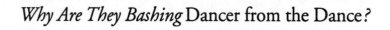

Why Are They Bashing Dancer from the Dance*?*

7

<hr/>

Why Are They Bashing Dancer from the Dance*?*

<hr/>

Published in 1978, Andrew Holleran's *Dancer from the Dance* was widely acclaimed in the gay and straight press for its vision, insight, humor, and sensuous prose. This tragicomic story of a hypnotically beautiful lawyer's obsessive failed search for love in seventies gay New York has sold steadily ever since, testimony to its power and originality. But three high-profile gay writers have recently attacked *Dancer* as seriously flawed and even dangerous: Bruce Bawer, David Leavitt, and Ethan Mordden. Given their reputations—and *Dancer from the Dance*'s renown—this criticism demands our scrutiny.[1]

Mordden levels several charges at *Dancer* in the introduction to his new anthology of gay fiction, *Waves*. Holleran's style is his first target: Mordden calls it "sloppy." It's a fascinating complaint, since reviewers have generally lavished praise on just that element of Holleran's novel. Mordden's examples of sloppy style? Holleran apparently spends too much time repeating images like "painter's jeans" and "T-shirts," "as if they were summoning terms of a ferocious power." Oh.

His assessment of *Dancer*'s character Sutherland as a "caricature" is clearer: "One of those inventions that seem based more on Eve Arden than on anyone in real life." But this claim is not substantiated. More damning for Mordden, however, are Holleran's "cultural gaffes" in *Dancer*: confusing John Quincy Adams with his father and spelling a singer's name wrong (Patti Joe rather than Patti Jo). If these errors strike you as trivial, they don't hit Mordden in the same way at all. To him, they reveal the pretensions of an "over-achiever." And he adduces other errors from Holleran's *Christopher Street* columns (but not from *Dancer*) as evidence. There's a misquotation from *King Lear*, as well as inaccurate references to *The Golden Bowl* and *Uncle Tom's Cabin*. These cultural gaffes point to flaws Mordden finds common in the informal gay writing group the Violet Quill, of which Holleran was a member: preciousness, and vanity triumphant over "good writing."

Having been the victim of bad copyediting myself, I would be loath to assume that spelling errors and even confusions about names are necessarily an author's fault. Conversely, since I've never really worked under the heavy pressure of writing a regular column, I don't know what mistakes might creep into copy I produced under deadline. Mordden's complaints along these lines amount to little more than nit-picking, just as his assessment of Holleran as an "over-achiever" and cultural gaffer seems like low-key character assassination.

It's also perilous to accuse a writer of cultural gaffes and then to make one yourself. Mordden lists Larry Kramer as a Violet Quill writer. As many readers might have noticed, Kramer does not appear in David Bergman's compendium *The Violet Quill Reader*, and I can't recall anyone ever mentioning Kramer as part of that group, including Kramer himself.

David Leavitt shifts the grounds of Holleran's literary misdemeanors from the textual to the psychosexual, so his reading of *Dancer from the Dance* is more entertaining, if more peculiar. In the introduction to his recent Penguin anthology of gay fiction, Leavitt recounts how in 1977, as a high school junior, he discovered gay fiction with Gordon Merrick's overripe *The Lord Won't*

Mind. Merrick's work left him both turned on and bewildered because he wondered if "sex between men [was] the exclusive property of the beautiful, the muscular, the superhuman."

Dancer was the second gay novel he read, and Holleran's novel was apparently quite traumatic for young Leavitt, even more devastating than *The Lord Won't Mind.* It "horrified" Leavitt because it seemed to say that the "only choices for gay men" were either to demonstrate "Chilly perfection. Inaccessibility. Disinterest"—or to "suffer from these unpleasant qualities." *Dancer* left Leavitt facing his future "with a kind of ashen horror" because he read it as premising a gay world in which "only the most exceptionally beautiful gay men were entitled to erotic fulfillment."

In slamming *Dancer,* Leavitt positions himself as the champion of a silent gay majority. He quotes a young friend who applauded his plans to "take on" Holleran's sacred cow: "Thank God someone's doing it. . . . It's the first gay book most young American gay men read, and I can't think of another that's done as much damage." For gay men coming out and searching for their identity, *Dancer from the Dance* is thus apparently little better than poison in its romanticization of what Leavitt calls "the dreariest aspect of gay experience": rejection, longing, worship of physical beauty. Leavitt does admit that the book is ironic "in some subtle way," though it's not clear if he made this point to his outraged friend.

Dancer was not just deeply disturbing to Leavitt because it seemed to deny him the chance of happiness as a gay man. It was a grave disappointment because he wanted a book "that told something like the truth"; he wanted "decent gay literature." That latter desire was one reason he started writing his first novel, *The Lost Language of Cranes,* in 1984, when he still knew little about gay literature.

This last note of Leavitt's is perplexing. The late seventies saw a great expansion of gay titles, and his lament of being limited to Gordon Merrick and Andrew Holleran seems disingenuous.

Even as a graduate of Yale, where there was a vital gay scene and one would assume people read books, Leavitt was apparently unfamiliar with the fiction of James Baldwin, Gore Vidal, Tennessee Williams, John Horne Burns, William S. Burroughs, and Christopher Isherwood—to mention some of the best known gay authors. Also widely available in paperback in the late seventies—when he was being shocked and traumatized—were such gay anthologies as *Different* and *The Other Persuasion,* as well as Roger Austen's history of American gay fiction, *Playing the Game.* Gay writing was neither invisible nor inaccessible, whether in bookstores or libraries.

Leavitt admits that in 1984 he didn't even know the posthumously published gay stories of E. M. Forster (published in *The Life to Come*). Presumably he didn't know of Forster's *Maurice,* either. How could an emerging gay literary figure have been so unaware? I wonder if he ever bothered browsing in bookstores, where all these writers, and many more, were widely available—and not just in gay sections. Did he read magazines, newspapers, book reviews? Did he read *Christopher Street,* which interviewed him when his first book came out? There may be more truth than I imagined in a phrase in Christopher Bram's review of Leavitt's *While England Sleeps,* that Leavitt has a "curiously inexperiencing nature."[2] How else can we explain that Leavitt lived in a veritable gay fiction–free zone not just in the late seventies, but the early eighties, too?

Bruce Bawer's reaction to *Dancer* in *A Place at the Table,* a plea for acceptance by mainstream America mixed with a harsh critique of "ghetto gays," is by far the most nuanced and considered of the three. Perhaps that is because of his conflicting responses. On one hand, he finds some truth in a book he calls "thoughtful" and "a remarkable piece of work: wistful, evocative, beautifully written." Bawer goes so far as to say that *Dancer* "might fairly be described as moral fiction"—despite "its grubby anecdotes about sex"—because it asks how gay men should live their lives.

But as Bawer sees it, the book's answer to that crucial question is deeply troubling and distorted. For Bawer, Holleran presents gay life as a curse, a doom, a sordid carnival of promiscuity. The only other choice is repression, dullness, conventionality, and shame. In other words, the closet. Because the novel "seriously" explores only "the most confused and wayward" gay men, it "implies that such gays represent the essence, the apotheosis, of gayness."

There's a strange naïveté in assuming, as Bawer does, that a novel's "domain" is proffered as a blueprint of life, or in expecting a novel to present a wide array of choices. Isn't one attraction of novels the immersion in a vision *unlike* your own? The chance to voyage into what *Dancer's* Sutherland says of New York's gay life, "a vast, uncharted continent"? And don't we expect novels to be different from debates?

Bawer's argument is undercut by his own admission that Holleran frames his novel with a series of ironic letters that "are plainly designed to put the novel's story in perspective." In fact, the letters announce the book's subject with a veritable fanfare. The story will be about "doomed queens" living in "the hothouse, artificial, desperate" environment of gay New York: "The Fags who consider themselves worthless because they are queer, and who fall into degradation and sordidness!" Bawer calls the presence of this contextualizing narrative frame in the book "little short of remarkable." Having condemned what he considers Holleran's narrow view of gay life, he is clearly at a loss to place the book's own clear criticism of such a view. Bawer falls back on the rhetoric of surprise, as if the framing letters were not an integral part of the novel's design and meaning. Holleran has said quite clearly that "*Dancer* was meant as an expose, a satire." I'm well aware that D. H. Lawrence warns us "Never trust the artist. Trust the tale." In this case, however, Holleran and his tale are in agreement.[3]

Further dismissing the power and significance of the letters, Bawer also worries that "it's too easy for a casual reader to miss [their] point . . . and to fail to realize that the narrator is intended to be unreliable." This is a very idiosyncratic concern. As an author and literary critic, I confess I have rarely worried about how "casual readers" might respond to my own fiction, or anyone else's. Is that who we should be writing for? Should our novels bear warning labels: "PAY ATTENTION — DON'T SKIM"?

Bawer does not seem to be personally devastated by *Dancer from the Dance* as David Leavitt was, nor is he as dismissive as Ethan Mordden. There is something almost elegiac in his comments about the novel, as if he regrets that so much talent could be used to such an inglorious and meretricious end. Bawer is not a novelist, however, so Holleran isn't his competition, and that may be why he doesn't slam the book by dishing Holleran, criticizing *Dancer's* style, or declaring the book toxic. But all three authors seem intent on shooting *Dancer from the Dance* out of the contemporary gay canon.

Will they succeed? Will more authors join in and condemn *Dancer* for misrepresenting gay life, for supposedly offering gay readers doom, gloom, sex, and cynicism? Will other critics ignore the main character's deep disillusionment with his life? Will the book's irony be vitiated by claims that it's "mad, bad, and dangerous" to read? Are we witnessing the beginning of some kind of gay backlash against *Dancer from the Dance?* And if so, why now, when gay books are more widely available from mainstream presses than ever before? What has led these three successful and established writers to mount their separate assaults on Castle Holleran? What do they have to gain by branding *Dancer from the Dance* as sloppy, horrifying, limited, untruthful, indecent?

Mordden, Leavitt, and Bawer's assessments puzzled me when I first encountered them because I have long considered *Dancer* not just a great gay book, but one of the most wrenching and powerful novels of obsession ever written. Rich in human understanding and passion, it brings to mind both *The Great Gatsby* and *The*

Alexandria Quartet in its style, characterization, and hypnotic narrative power. I have never read it as offering me a prescription for how to live my life as a gay man, but as offering savage insight into the ways *some* gay men have lived.

The message I first found in *Dancer from the Dance* was not "You're doomed," but, "Try writing a gay novel as good as this." I was excited and challenged by the possibility, and enriched by the book's very existence. I felt the same sense of discovery and exaltation reading and rereading *Dancer* as when I encountered amazing books by Anne Tyler, James Baldwin, Virginia Woolf, Philip Roth, Henry James, Joan Didion, Aharon Appelfeld, Dorothy Allison, D. H. Lawrence, Jean Rhys, Alan Hollinghurst, Anita Brookner, Don DeLillo, and Julian Barnes. With each, I felt a whole new universe of feeling and observation had opened up to me, changing me not just as a man or a gay man, but as a writer.

More than any other, Holleran's novel sets a dazzling standard for contemporary gay literature. Its recent critics remind me of Oscar Wilde's observation that "those who find ugly meanings in beautiful things are corrupt without being charming. This is a fault."

Notes

1. Quotations are from *Waves: An Anthology of New Gay Fiction*, ed. Ethan Mordden (New York: Vintage, 1994); *The Penguin Book of Gay Short Stories*, David Leavitt and Mark Mitchell, eds., with an introduction by David Leavitt (New York: Viking, 1994); Bruce Bawer, *A Place at the Table: The Gay Individual in American Society* (New York: Poseidon, 1993); and Andrew Holleran, *Dancer from the Dance* (New York: Plume, 1986; originally published by Morrow, 1978).

2. Christopher Bram, "Arrested Innocence," a review of *While England Sleeps* by David Leavitt. *Lambda Book Report* 4 (November/December 1993), 26–27.

3. Andrew Holleran, in the tenth-anniversary reissue of *Dancer from the Dance* (New York: Morrow, 1988), 4. D. H. Lawrence, *Studies in Classic American Literature* (New York: Penguin, 1978), 8.

Selling Was Never My Line

8

Selling Was Never My Line

As a shy, somewhat overweight, sexually confused teenager with bad teeth, I hated working at my father's little store in New York's Washington Heights. I felt exposed and embarrassed. I was bad at arithmetic and panicky at the cash register when people said things like, "I have a nickel." I had no idea what they meant.

I swore to myself that when I grew up, I would never do retail. But that's exactly what happened when I launched a book tour that led to over one hundred readings and signings promoting my collection *Dancing on Tisha B'Av* and my novel *Winter Eyes.* I've read at bookstores, synagogues, universities, Jewish community centers, and writers' conferences—from Pittsburgh to Paris.

Along the way, I've probably met (and forgotten the names of) more people while touring than I have met in my entire lifetime. I've completely overcome my feelings of "I don't get out enough." I've earned tens of thousands of frequent-flyer miles. I know the way to the Lansing airport in my sleep. I've gone deeply into debt, and I feel as dazed and bedraggled as Agnes Gooch in *Auntie Mame* realizing that she's "lived."

It all started innocently enough at the 1990 Out/Write, the first national conference of lesbian and gay writers. I was blissfully floating in a sea of writers, publishers, editors, and journalists, and meeting people I wanted to meet and some who wanted to meet me. I was enjoying the excitement of starting something new, of being part of a vibrant community. I was also relishing the parade of men and the gay fashion statements that wouldn't even be fashion whispers in my mid-Michigan town.

During one morning address, Michael Denneny, my editor at St. Martin's Press at the time, was urging writers to actively help build their own careers. A publisher can't create an audience, Denneny said; a writer has to do that, and by doing readings. It made perfect sense to me. I was electrified by the idea of not being passive when my book of short stories came out the following fall. Instead of waiting to see what my publisher would do and what might happen, I could take steps myself, take charge. I turned to Gersh and said, "We can do that, can't we?"

I suppose he could have slapped me, or said, "I'm busy this decade," or just pretended not to hear me. But he got excited too, and so our combination bake sale/crusade began. We had no idea what was in store.

At readings, being handed checks or cash by mistake has made me very uncomfortable, although I haven't had to make change. When people inviting me to come read at their schools or synagogues ask me to bring copies of my books, I'm instantly reminded of one of my parents' friends, Mr. Sorkin, a shirt salesman. I picture myself burdened with a huge, black, wheeled sample case . . .

In the beginning, when I showed up at a bookstore, I expected an attractive or at least visible window display, with a sign of some kind and artfully arranged copies of my book. But sometimes there was almost nothing, or what was in the window was so boring and unappealing I felt like I was looking at a window display for trusses, walkers, and orthopedic hose.

At one store, Gersh squinted at a dreary arrangement of my books atop a low bookcase and suddenly started rearranging it like a jaunty chef on a TV cooking show. In a few minutes, the display was attractive and eye-catching. He shrugged at my surprise. "Somebody had to do it," he said matter-of-factly.

Equally as disappointing as poor displays, at first, was the ring of cash registers and phones. I learned that bookstores can't afford to close down for an hour or even a half-hour while an author reads. Just as strange as the noise was having browsers idle right by while I read, either not looking, or looking and listening for a bit, and then moving on. I felt publicly branded as boring.

At one bookstore I was squeezed into a corner formed by two long shelves—making the point of a triangle. I felt claustrophobic and trapped, and worried what my body looked like in perspective. Even worse was reading in a bookstore in front of a wall of erotic greeting cards.

There have been other discomforts. My collection's title has Hebrew in it, referring to the Jewish fast day that memorializes the Roman destruction of the Temple in Jerusalem. That Hebrew can lead to trouble when I'm introduced. *Dancing on Tisha B'Av* has been called "Dancing on Tisha B'Avenue," "Dancing on Tisha Bay," "Dancing on Tisha Baja," "Dancing on Trisha B'Av," and even "Dancing on the Tissue Box."

Before reading a story, I like to talk about coming out as a gay man and as a Jewish man, and afterward I like to take questions. So I give out a lot of information about myself—which probably encourages readers to assume the stories are even more autobiographical than they might in fact be. This has led to odd interactions. Because one of my Jewish characters is uncircumcised, someone asked if *I* was. I told him to check with my editor.

Most people are less intrusive when they speak to me after a reading and ask me to sign their books, although I was thrown by the enthusiastic reader who demanded I write something funny in Yiddish in her book; I ended up barely able to write in English. Occasionally someone will gush over my work and then compare me to Writer X, whom I despise. I've learned to smile and just say thanks.

"Why should I buy this book?" some people have asked at bookstores, and I'm generally dumbfounded. The best response was offered by a witty friend after a reading from *Dancing on Tisha B'Av* at Lambda Rising in Washington, D.C. He pointed out to a hesitant buyer, "Really, the hardcover's a bargain at sixteen ninety-five—that's only about ninety cents a story."

And a sale was made, but I decided then and there that my second collection would have no story under a dollar.

I've been asked to prove that my book has "something to say to women," and have been chastised for writing about people "unfamiliar" to the reader. Being gay and Jewish has also led to a confusion of identities. Dining with sponsors of my reading at a New England university, I was surprised when a latecomer gushed, "I loved *Equal Affections*!" "That's by David Leavitt," I pointed out as the table fell silent. "I'm Lev Raphael." Plunging ahead, the woman said, "Oh, but both of you are gay and Jewish, right?" Someone else at the table piped up, "Well, that's true, but in Lev's fiction, you can *tell*."

But despite some bizarre and even dispiriting experiences out on the road, the tour was mostly positive, even exciting in ways I couldn't have imagined. Reading a story for an audience, I enter it in a completely different way, inhabiting it now, whereas before it inhabited me. I listen to myself with a double consciousness—examining how I respond to the story when read aloud, and how others respond. I see that some lines don't work as well as I thought, and some scenes play better than I realized. I edit as I read, and each reading teaches me how to tackle the next one.

Doing retail *could* be worse.

Scars

I couldn't ever seem to learn where my father's edge was;
one step on terra firma, the next off and tumbling into space.

The Duke of Deception
GEOFFREY WOLFF

9

Scars

I

My father even criticized the way I walked and stood. Out on the street—out on Broadway. "Walk like *this*." And he'd put his feet out train-track straight, stride and march.

One hundred fiftieth Street and Broadway, Harlem now, Washington Heights when I grew up. How many people watched him stop me and demonstrate?

Was I pigeon-toed? I can't remember which way my feet were turned. But they weren't turned his way. I didn't walk like him. I wasn't him—was that his gripe?

Or, leaning against a counter or a wall, my feet turned in, balanced on each inner edge—I liked how it felt—he'd badger me to stand up straight. Was it bad for my flat feet? For my shoes? I never understood. That was the problem. I couldn't understand his rules, his standards, his demands.

As a little boy I was mystified by cars, by my father in a car. He demanded we stop talking when he turned the key in the ignition, as if our silence protected us—or him—like goggles from the glare of an atomic test. What did it mean? What did any of them mean, these crazy rules?

115

Thirty-five years later, he hasn't changed. Watches me pouring milk over cereal. Under his eye, I pour too much, of course.

Flatly he says, "Oh. You like so much milk?"

Well, not always, but see, I forgot to use my measuring cup to get the right proportion of flake to liquid . . . My smart-ass retort goes unshared. Instead, I reply as if he's asked a sensible and interesting question, as if we're having a conversation and I'm not on trial.

Another time, a few years earlier. I'm in my thirties, at my parents' cramped and grimy Forest Hills kitchen where the glossy walls are flecked with stove-top grease. He watches me empty an ice tray on a narrow counter. "That's how you do it?" Almost always there's a question that implies I'm wrong. Almost always, I want to flare up, but stifle my annoyance. Sometimes I can laugh, imagine that he's kidding me.

These small domestic moments are continual episodes in my disgrace. I never meet his expectations, whatever they are. Even when I do well, he finds a way to savage my composure.

In college, acting in *Measure for Measure,* enjoying myself. His only comment is, "How come he walks so quietly on the stage? At home, he's like an elephant."

Yes, that's me, noisy, clumsy, loud, unathletic, the old me buried today under the well-built man who lifts weights, talks about trainers, food programs, protein, vascularity and body composition. The bullied little boy is along for the ride, glad of my protection.

II

A *vildeh chaya,* he called me, a "wild animal" in Yiddish, because I was loud, defiant, sarcastic. When he spanked me, I screamed so much I made him sick, ashamed. Knowing his weakness, unconsciously (and loving to make noise), I screamed before he even touched me, ran screaming down the long hallway to hide under my bed, where he'd have to drag me out.

116

My mother found my racket comforting. "I always knew where you were in the house when you were little." And we smiled at this.

But my father called me "stupid" because of my noise, my silliness, my aping what he said and how he said it. I was dramatically defiant. Unlike my brother Sam, whose revolutions skulked behind a placid wall—vandalism, fighting, drugs.

His nickname for me, "Stupid," became a brand, so ineradicable that in my freshman year of college, I called Kris, the first professor to ever give me an A, to find out if she really thought I deserved it.

And not just "stupid." In English: "A mouth like a garbage can." I was disgusted but pleased—the cans I thought of were big and steel and hard to crush.

"Azah moyl"—Such a mouth—but the translation doesn't capture his dry contempt.

And even now, despite the years of public speaking, I can wonder after a party (even my own): Did I talk too much?

III

Was I an angry child? My mother said I sang and smiled. She also said I threw wooden figures from the Belgian Congo out my bedroom window. I remember pissing in the metal kitchen garbage can, the echoed hit and hiss. I poured salt into *latkes* frying on the stove and spoiled their taste.

I was an angry adolescent, cursing, screaming at my brother who seemed as tyrannical as my father, but unfairly. Wasn't he also a son?

Am I angry now? Unfair?

Because my father must have laughed with me, at least when I was very young and bathed with him, and splashed.

Is all of this a settling of accounts, now that his face is eating through my own?

My mother said that boys my age who came into the store looked up to him, sought his advice.

I never did.

IV

Describing him is difficult. There is his general effect on me: intimidation, envy, shame. There is the slightly pathetic older man he has become. There is the recent immigrant of my childhood, the man staring out impassive from one 1950s black and white Kodak after another, unsmiling giant of my youth (though never tall). Bright red hair, gray eyes, freckles, with the build and hard, brooding handsomeness of Dana Andrews. (Is that why *Laura* has such a hold on me?) Is it my own fantasy that my father, mostly cold, was a warm and passionate man inside, smitten, moved?

With crude poetry, this is how he described meeting my mother in Germany after World War II, after their concentration camps were liberated: "I saw her. She was mine, I was hers." Nothing else.

Hearing this, I was too young and stunned to even ask what he meant. Their love was fated? Immediate? Or—they had sex? That day, that week? I see a picture of them on a Belgian beach, standing side by side, and he is closer to the lens. His swim suit bulges, her breasts are large and full.

Who is this man who chose a German Shepherd as his dog? A gentle dog, but he named it Rippy, Rip.

What could it mean to walk this dog, to feed and brush and bathe the type of dog the Germans used against men like him? Surely dogs like this had growled and snarled at him, threatened to rip his throat apart. And now he led one on a leash, now he was the master.

I have written about him again and again, reflections, shards. The opening of my first published story:

Marc's father had an odd, stubborn way of standing: His hands were inevitably in his pockets and all of him seemed to lean forward, as if he'd placed himself in your path and the next move were up to *you*. In his father's presence Marc often felt as if he had to excuse himself; one look of those narrow grey eyes would put him so much on the defensive that even a "hello" could come out apologetically. Ten minutes alone with his father could exhaust Marc. Luckily, his father rarely spoke to him.

Reading this now, it seems too tame. No hint of thuggery, no sneers, no shaking disappointed head. Back then, perhaps I thought there'd come a time when we could talk, be close, and so I muffled who he was.

In those 1950s snapshots he looks sullen, maybe trapped. But why?

I'm nineteen when he reveals he wanted to leave us many times. But my brother topped that revelation years later: "Dad told me he wanted to jump in the Hudson when they got to New York—he couldn't take it." Escaping us? My mother? Or just life? These bombs of truth flatten me.

V

My father has left me scarred. There's a photo of the four of us, I'm an infant, plastic nipple in my mouth, bandage across my head, lying in my mother's arms. She looks down, and smiles. My father stands apart, in short-sleeved shirt and pleated pants. The story: My mother said she asked him to put me to bed, several times, because I looked tired. I fell somehow against the glass-topped blond wood coffee table, ripping open an eyebrow, needing stitches. I have the scar—a line, a space where nothing grows. I see that fifties room—the archway to the foyer, the double French doors to the dining room, the smaller one to the hall. The olive rug, the thick and heavy chairs and couch, in green or red shot through with gold; the bulky matching drapes and ugly driftwood lamps. I see it all, but have no memories. I have the scar.

Domestic and Space Invaders

10

Domestic and Space Invaders

Andrew Bergman and Eugene Stein's new books fully prove Tolstoy's much-quoted observation that "each unhappy family is unhappy in its own way." Both novelists show us Jewish families almost burst apart by the secrets, deception, and even madness at their core.

Best known for comedies like *Soapdish, Blazing Saddles,* and *Honeymoon in Vegas,* writer-director Andrew Bergman charts very different territory in *Sleepless Nights.* The novel is a haunting and hypnotic study of a claustrophobic family of German-Jewish refugees whose son Robby spends half his life fighting free of childhood sexual victimization.

The Weisglass apartment "in darkest Queens" is like a tiny threatened outpost in a hostile land, driven in on itself. It's a home of vigilance, strange silences, and panics—and anger is as rare in this home "as an epileptic fit, and is perceived in roughly the same way—as an attack."

Refugees from Nazi Germany, the Weisglasses seem stripped of history and order, which leaves chaos reigning in a stifling environment where the "secrets are as copious as termites." "Things We Don't Discuss" are raised "and then dropped without explanation."

One of Robby Weisglass's girlfriends aptly describes his parents as acting like spies: "'The level of secrecy, it's unbearable. Everything is unspoken.'"

Growing up, Robby shares a room with his older sister, Carol, a shameless and stunning lingerie model who likes him to watch her undress, and who has sexual contact with him until his bar mitzvah, when she cheerfully gives him his freedom. But this undiscussed incest is fairly positive for Robby compared to the frightening assaults his mother makes on him, driven by her own inexplicable demons.

Robby is not only haunted by the sex with his mother, he's haunted by the way she has seemingly filled every corner of his life. His mother claims with terrifying believability that she knows him better than he knows himself. "She was godlike," he reflects, and then adds with characteristic wit, "bigger than God actually, because God never cooked for me."

Sleepless Nights powerfully weaves the past and the present together as Robby, a history professor at Columbia, tries to exorcise his family's hold on him in therapy. Feeling contaminated by his mother's molestation, how can he have good relationships with women, and, more pressingly, how can he ever become a father? His own father has been absent and uninvolved; his mother has offered a bizarre parental model, claiming that she acted out of love for him, and he'll understand when he has kids. Robby has fantasies of being a father, but he's terrified of imposing himself on his children the way his mother suffocated him.

Robby's sister Carol knows there's a way out, and her advice to Robby late in the book echoes some aspects of the situation of many children of Holocaust survivors: "If you focus on what [our parents] went through, then you make yourself responsible for everything." It will take Robby twenty years of therapy and suffering to drag himself out of the tar pit of his family's past, to accept his parents' terrible pain as beyond him to resolve, and find love and security with a young Jewish woman whose history is similarly dark and tortured. Their joint victory is dazzling and unforgettable.

One of the many triumphs in this memorable book is the absolute authority with which Bergman creates the feel of a refugee community. Suspicious, fearful, terrorized by the past, they cling to a sense of superiority. Friendship as Americans see it is completely alien to them because they believe that only people without a family need friends. These refugees are perpetually aware that they have escaped, and many are damaged beyond repair, though outwardly functional. All of them have what Robby describes as the "classic refugee look: eyes radiating curiosity, suspicion, and neediness."

But Bergman also sees the fiercely comic side of refugee life. Robby's Tante Bertha is typical because "she fancies herself an expert on road conditions and navigation" even though she's never driven a car. And Robby's mother shouts into telephones because "she doesn't entirely believe that telephonic communication has been perfected."

Robby shares their profound sense of always being outsiders, and tells his analyst that the feelings predate his mother's incest. He's an outsider in the world, and in his own family. He never really talks with his father, just listens to his father's anecdotes and asks the same questions each time: "It is like having a conversation, with none of the risk." But his parents' stories about their suffering in Germany and the deaths of their family leave him deeply traumatized. As a little boy he is even afraid to go to school, because it reminds him of Auschwitz, "with its steel fencing, its vast, dim, sinister basement, its thundering furnace and steadily spewing smokestack." The revelation of this sickening fear, and his parents' response to it, is a tour de force of tension and anguish.

In another register, the Weisglass family's alienation leads to one of the most comically poignant set pieces of the book when the family of four spends a week at a restricted 1950s summer resort because Robby's father is there to write a vacation review for a magazine. The Weisglasses act like "four quarrelsome paratroopers dropped behind enemy lines." Dinner is "a gastronomic nightmare . . . things in aspic, boiled vegetables, puff pastries. Anti-Semitism in edible form."

The novel is structured around a series of Robby's sessions with his analyst, and they are deeply moving and often very funny. At the beginning, for instance, Robby is very suspicious, even contemptuous: "The whole concept is so banal—this registering of feelings, one by one, like beads on an abacus. You put them together, they don't add up to shit." By the time his analysis is over, readers can feel as tearful and impressed as his analyst. Bergman manages to avoid the clichés of such scenes, mostly through his keen ear for dialogue. It's the pungent, strong, affecting dialogue throughout that helps make what might seem an unbelievable situation not only real but completely compelling and never prurient. Bergman's beautifully written novel is an important addition to the growing body of fiction by and about children of Holocaust survivors.

Straitjacket & Tie, Eugene Stein's sad and sometimes farcical first novel, offers an intriguing layering of themes. At its core, the novel studies the devastation that mental illness wreaks on the Rosenbaum family. Stein subtly counterpoints this drama with the younger Rosenbaum son's search for sexual identity and commitment, and the strength to ask for what he wants. But most originally, the book's cast of eccentrics includes some very colorful— and Jewish-friendly—aliens from the Planet Debbie. That's right, Debbie.

These aliens are unlike any you've ever met, and they almost walk—or fly—away with the novel. They're not cuddly like ET, or menacing like the Terminator. They're by turns raucous, raunchy, avuncular, drug-loving, given to pronouncements, and definitely *heymish.* Fascinated by American pop culture, they are also completely invisible.

Well, almost. They *can* be seen by dogs, Scandinavians, and twins, among others. These Debbie-ites knit, smoke, do their nails, quote Carole King and Oscar Wilde, watch "Star Trek," sport Norma Kamali outfits, love Robin Williams and Gary Cooper, can sing in Yiddish, have children with names like Shulamith, and throw around words familiar from Russian-Jewish life like *babba* (granny) and *malchick* (young boy). There's more: These oily, fishy space travelers are also omnisexual and look like fuzzy green lawn chairs.

In a delightful turnaround, Stein's alien crew does not descend on a terrorized motorist along a plains state highway, or swoop down on a gaping little kid in a farmer's field. They materialize to a nice Jewish boy from the Bronx. Bert Rosenbaum encounters them in New York's Riverside Park, at Coliseum Books near Columbus Circle, and in the air shaft of an Upper West Side building. Their role in the book is choral: They comment on and kibbitz about earth's extraordinary level of violence, its weird notions of what sexuality is, and the inability on Earth "to communicate with the insane," a problem that has deep personal meaning for Bert Rosenbaum.

Bert is a somewhat subdued 1982 Princeton graduate stuck in a boring civil service job for the Department of Sewers, who has feared madness and sometimes courted it. His idolized older brother Philip went crazy when Bert was sixteen, and Philip's schizophrenia is movingly drawn, both in itself and how it frightens and demoralizes Bert and his parents. Both Mr. and Mrs. Rosenbaum will always wonder—quite fruitlessly—what they might have done differently as parents, how they could have kept Philip sane.

The mother is a typist studying pharmacy, and the father is a typesetter. So it is intriguing that Philip's madness is defiantly logocentric. He inappropriately bursts into quotations from Bob Dylan songs and TV shows in public, and writes disjointed poetry. One of Philip's major delusions is imagining that Dylan's songs contain a secret message just for him. More chillingly for his younger brother, Bert, Philip is initially convinced of a conspiracy by homosexuals to take over the planet, using secret broadcasts "to make people gay." Philip's disgust for homosexuality changes in the course of the novel, but well before that it deadens Bert's awareness of his own attraction to men. And worse, that disgust makes Bert's longing seem more disruptive, threatening, and dangerous. It's impossible for Bert, who is "such a good boy," to tell his parents about his feelings for men, since the seismic waves of Philip's madness have shaken Mr. and Mrs. Rosenbaum too much. There's no emotional room in this family for another burden, another trauma.

One of the novel's strengths is Stein's portrayal of the deep connection between brothers that can sour for so many reasons. Like many younger brothers, Bert has longed to *be* Philip, and so his brother's madness is a tragedy for Bert, burying both the boy he admired and much of their shared history.

Stein beautifully captures the helplessness, heartbreak, and unexpected ambivalence of watching someone you love disappear forever into madness, become changed and—yes—alien. At one point after Mrs. Rosenbaum has earned her pharmacy degree, she plaintively tells Bert: "I'm fifty-six years old, I've been working a long time. I just wanted some peace and quiet . . . I love him, and I want him to get better. Every day I give people pills and cure them, and I think, why can't I cure my own son? But I come home at night and I'm scared. I don't want him here . . . am I such a terrible mother?"

Stein also understands the profound shame about mental illness in one's family which can silence you, make you withdraw from others, or at least feel cut off, afraid of exposing family secrets. The perverse opposite is also part of the situation. Bert can use his brother's madness as a conversational ploy to make himself interesting. And of course Philip's madness is interesting—a whole strange little universe of its own that can be terrifying in its intensity (as when Philip throws family belongings out the window) and weirdly funny. Early on, resisting his parents' efforts to send him to a psychiatrist, Philip admits to "having some minor emotional problems, but as soon as the Yankees met the Mets in a subway series, all his problems would disappear; it was no use trying to get him to see a psychiatrist — they should try to get the Mets some decent pitching."

Through most of the novel, we follow Bert as he drifts through school, is visited by the aliens, ambivalently attracted to women at work and in business school, drawn to men who cannot love him, and most significantly, haunted by his brother's mental illness, which gets deeper and more difficult for the Rosenbaums to cope with. His first lover reminds him of Philip, an uneasy connection. "What if all this time, Philip and gay desire had lurked inside him, dormant, like a slow virus?"

While Bert drifts, Philip deteriorates steeply and painfully, with escalating and interminable wrangling over his medication. Eventually he is hospitalized. Bert has shared his room and his life with Philip for far too long, and near the end of the novel he finally lets go of his fear of being crazy himself. He starts dating a man who is not ambivalent or given to mind games. Liberated and relieved, Bert can reclaim the sweet and touching memories of loving a brother.

And the aliens? After a bout with drug abuse, recovery, and doctoral work, pregnancy takes them back to Debbie. Throughout the book they have had some of the best lines and observations, like noting the hidden sadomasochism in children's board games. Their departure is no exception. They predict that in addition to gay rights becoming "universal," there will be a woman president who is "queer, black, Jewish." And a former astronaut, yet.

Stein's sly references in *Straitjacket & Tie* to Henry James's *The Ambassadors* point to the heart of the book. Twice Bert complains about the James novel as boring and soporific, hard to read, yet he has a discovery scene similar to the famous one in which Lambert Strether comes across Mme. de Vionnet and Chad boating on a river, obviously lovers, though they have led him to believe otherwise. Passing a hotel, Bert runs into coworkers Patrick (whom he's slept with) and Diana (whom he's flirted with). Realizing that they are having an affair and trying to cover it up, he senses a resemblance to something he's read.

The connection is deeper than this playful echo. Despite the aliens, the mental illness, and all the other bizarre scenes and people in *Straitjacket & Tie*, Bert's ultimate change is very Jamesian. At the end of *The Ambassadors*, trying to understand what he returns to in America after all his mental adventures in France, Strether agrees that he is going back to "a great difference." Stein's achievement in this likable and comic novel is to make that difference real and convincing, and to remind us that shifts of consciousness are sometimes the strangest and most fulfilling voyages we make.

Judaism's Moral Strength

11

Judaism's Moral Strength

As a writer and avid magazine and newspaper reader, I've always liked to follow opinions and controversies in the letters columns of journals I read. I enjoy well-argued letters and the unexpected tidbits of information I sometimes learn from knowledgeable letter writers. But reading letters to the editor in the *Lansing State Journal,* our local paper, is often a depressing and maddening experience for me. The voices of narrow-mindedness, ignorance, and unadulterated hatred crop up far too frequently, making me feel isolated.

I'm thinking of a recent letter in the *Lansing State Journal* in which someone confidently maintained that the persecution of Jews and homosexuals in—as she confusedly put it—"postwar" Germany could not be compared. Why? Because Jews were persecuted for being Jewish, while homosexuals were persecuted for "illegal and immoral behavior."

That letter writer seemed to imply that the persecution of homosexuals—which included harassment, incarceration in concentration camps, torture, and death—is acceptable. Or at least more acceptable than persecuting Jews.

To make such a statement is to blame the victim, and we Jews should be sensitive to such rhetorical tricks, since we have been falsely accused by some writers of having participated in our own slaughter during World War II, and even of having encouraged it in some obscene way.

Thousands of homosexuals were persecuted and murdered by the Nazis because the Nazis were sick and full of hate. It is the behavior and identity of the *murderers* that counts, not the victims, because the Nazis targeted different groups for discrimination, imprisonment, or death at different times: Jehovah's Witnesses, labor union leaders, epileptics, women, Catholics, Gypsies, Communists, the mentally retarded, Poles. Anyone could have been crushed by the Nazi Moloch for reasons of policy. Though Jews were always the Nazis' prime target, anyone could be made vulnerable and ruled outside of the law.

Yes, homosexual activity was illegal in Germany *before* Hitler. But the Nazis further restricted and punished it in their complete perversion of German law and life in which scapegoating and hounding Jews was paramount. In 1933 laws were passed to ban Jews from the legal professions and civil service; groups promoting homosexual rights were banned that same year. The 1935 Nuremberg laws eliminated Jews' civil rights and citizenship, and banned intermarriage and sexual contacts between Jews and non-Jews. That very year, widened restrictions on homosexuals, such as banning gay bars, made it more possible to legally target homosexuals for persecution. Conditions for German Jews grew steadily harsher and ended in catastrophe, but perhaps less well known—especially to Jews—is the parallel persecution of homosexuals. That sad history is well documented in books like Richard Plant's *The Pink Triangle,* praised by no less a writer than Holocaust historian Martin Gilbert.

It would be a mistake for me to sneeringly shrug off evidence of prejudice like that letter in the *Lansing State Journal* and say, "Well, that's Lansing, what can you expect from a town that thinks it's a city?" What can you expect from what my parents would pungently call in Yiddish a *lochovich* (a nowhere town)?

A real mistake. Because the bigoted voices I encounter in the *Lansing State Journal* are sometimes echoed in our supposedly more sophisticated and tolerant Jewish community. With no sense of history, letters in the *Detroit Jewish News* have called for death to homosexuals, as the Torah seems to urge.

The link of Jews and homosexuals is one that makes some Jews extremely uncomfortable. Understandably so, up to a point. When many Jews hear any other group mentioned as having been targeted in the Holocaust, they rightly fear that the specific nature of Jewish suffering and destruction will be blurred. That the Shoah will simply be classed as another example of human brutality, and Jews will suffer a second historical erasure.

But this fear can lead to bizarre and irrational behavior. To speak of Jews and homosexuals as victims of the Nazis does no dishonor to Jews, does not in any way decrease the significance of the catastrophe for Jews. Yet too many Jews recoil in disgust and horror, or get enraged when the subject comes up.

Jewish communities have historically encouraged and admired learning and wisdom, so it is particularly disturbing when Jews, of all people, parade ignorance and intolerance as knowledge. I had ample opportunity to observe aspects of this behavior when I toured the country in 1991 and 1992 promoting *Dancing on Tisha B'Av*.

In one city, I learned that organizers of a Holocaust memorial commemoration absolutely refused to allow a non-Jewish gay man to light one of the six memorial candles. The reasons were many but overlapping: It was not his place to be there, it was not appropriate, how could you say what happened to Jews and gays was the same? But the rage underneath these assertions was telling. How dare he put himself forward, how dare any homosexual claim the right to participate in this ceremony! I have attended Holocaust memorial ceremonies where a number of groups are listed along with Jews, but never homosexuals.

In another city, I ran into a wall when I spoke at a Jewish community center with Evelyn Torton Beck, editor of the groundbreaking *Nice Jewish Girls: A Lesbian Anthology.* She is the child of survivors, as I am, and she is a lesbian. I was dumbfounded when we met informally with a group of children of survivors who asked point-blank why we "had to be gay" that evening. Why couldn't we set it aside?

When you're in a Christian group, we asked, do you set your Jewishness aside, isn't that always a part of your identity?

They didn't see the connection. Our multiple identities as Jews, children of survivors, and homosexuals seemed to embarrass and even confuse them. And they wouldn't admit that the rabid hatred directed at lesbians and gays by some in the Jewish community *is* hatred.

"It's religion," they insisted, sounding as petulant to me as students defending an indefensible statement with the sullen claim, "It's my opinion, it doesn't have to be right."

Lies are lies. Hatred is hatred. As Jews, we know what it sounds and feels and smells and tastes like. Those of us who haven't experienced it directly know others who have.

And when a New York rabbi went to Oregon to support and defend the right-wing activists who wanted to enlist state government in limiting the rights of gays and lesbians and actively discouraging homosexuality—and he claimed religious authority—that, too, was hatred, plain and simple. This same rabbi claimed that comparing Oregon's Measure 9 to Nazi laws against the Jews was the act of "ignorant people." Clearly, his zealotry made him ignorant of what is indisputable historical fact: the Nazis' legal and murderous campaign of persecution against Jews *and* homosexuals.

Likewise, controversy recently erupted in Detroit's Jewish community about the whole question of rabbis performing commitment ceremonies for gay and lesbian Jews. Ridiculous and bigoted claims were made about gay and lesbian Jews and about homo-sexuality—by *rabbis,* our supposed leaders.

One rabbi said that homosexuals "define themselves by their sexuality." Another said that same-sex Jewish commitment cere-monies would promote "a lifestyle of instinctual gratification which is not channeled or sublimated toward a greater objective." In other, cruder words: All that gay people think about or want is sex; they have no life outside of sex.

This charge is exactly the same kind of vicious calumny that anti-Semites have historically directed at Jews: They say we're only interested in money. Both claims are absurd, disgusting, and dangerous, because they lead from stereotyping to violence of at-titude and action. Furthermore, calling gayness a "lifestyle" trivi-alizes something very complex (sexual identity), reducing it to faddishness.

These responses remind me of a poignant passage in Joseph Beam's black gay anthology *In the Life:*

> I cannot go home as who I am. When I speak of home, I mean not only the familial constellation from which I grew, but the entire Black community, the Black press, the Black church, Black acade-micians, the Black literati, and the Black left. Where is my reflec-tion? I am most often rendered invisible, perceived as a threat to the family, or am tolerated if I am silent and inconspicuous. I can-not go home as who I am and that hurts me deeply.

What, then, is the answer? Rabbi Michael Sternfield of Congre-gation Beth Israel in San Diego has dealt beautifully and clearly with outrageous and destructive Jewish claims about homosexual-ity. In an Erev Rosh Hashanah sermon, he urged his congregation:

> We need a Judaism which *includes;* a Judaism which is expansive and outreaching; a Judaism which recognizes the inherent dignity and worth in life of each person. This means that as a community,

we must do our very best to include not only gays and lesbians, but also *single* Jews, *poor* Jews, *divorced* Jews, Jews with *physical* and *mental* disabilities, Jews who are *intermarried*—in other words, all of those of our people who seem not to conform to the theoretical model. . . . Jews, better than most, should understand the bitterness of *ostracism, suspicion* and *phobias* for we have been strangers in many lands. . . . Our attitude towards gays and lesbians is a *true test* of the depth of our commitment to the Torah's human values. Judaism's moral strength is tested not by how narrowly we may define its parameters, but rather how broadly we can draw its circle.

Dangerous Men

12

Dangerous Men

We live in a Midwestern university community where we've taught at the university for almost forty years combined. Our four-bedroom ranch house is on a quiet tree-lined street in a comfortable suburb that was built up after World War II. We chat with our neighbors about the weather. We write letters to the editor of our local paper when we're moved by some issue, which is often. We know some of the reporters there, and women and men working in our post office by first name. We vote in every election and in primaries. We sometimes watch township meetings on cable TV, and keep track of township developments.

We worry about drugs in the high school, real estate taxes, local streets without enough stop signs, moles in the lawn, about gypsy moths and tent caterpillars, about dry summers that'll burn out lawns and winters with too much snow that will make the river flood in the spring. Much of our time is spent in undramatic pursuits like laundry, shopping, making minor home repairs, washing the cars, gardening, trimming trees and shrubs, mowing the lawn, raking leaves in the fall, and shoveling the driveway in the winter.

We've been raising two kids. Raising them has meant helping with homework, watching TV and going to movies together, shopping for clothes more often than we hoped to because the kids kept outgrowing things, attending parent-teacher conferences, stopping work to take one of them to the doctor, chauffeuring them to school activities and social groups, helping them learn to drive. It's also meant admiring their accomplishments and trying to remember that they're just kids and we need to be patient and forgiving when they mess up. We've been sharing with them our understanding of our religious and cultural inheritance, talking about moral and ethical dilemmas in their lives, our lives, and in our country.

We attended David's graduation from the University of Wisconsin this past winter, and helped him move into a new apartment in Madison. We supplied him with furniture in addition to the lamps, dishes, and bookcases from the attic we brought for his previous apartment. After a celebratory dinner, hugging good-bye was very emotional for all of us. This fall we've turned into a two-man writing workshop to help Aaron not only write college applications, but deal with an English teacher whose grasp of her material is shaky and who has no idea how to offer encouraging and stimulating suggestions about his compositions. We've spent many hours on his writing because it's so important.

Together, the four of us have rooted for Michigan State's football team, have gone to every home game, and almost always watched away games on TV or even listened to them on the radio. We've flown the Michigan State flag on game days and worn MSU buttons and MSU's colors, green and white. One year we even took the kids to the Rose Bowl and spent almost a week enjoying Southern California.

In many ways, we're a stereotypically American family. Except that my partner and I are both queer. And we're both Jewish, and we've been served a warning by the Republicans that this is not our country anymore.

At the 1992 Republican auto-da-fé in Houston, Patrick Buchanan, Pat Robertson, and other Defenders of the Faith declared war in no uncertain terms on people of color, women who think for themselves, feminists, Democrats, lesbians and gays, and Jews. Explicitly and implicitly, we were all branded as "un-American" and their glorious crusade is now to take back the cities, the culture, and the country that we have supposedly stolen from them.

It seems bizarrely appropriate that this sweeping series of condemnations and talk of "religious war" occurred on the five-hundredth-year anniversary of the Spanish expulsion of Jews and Moors, which capped Spain's years of efforts to make itself a pure and Catholic state. The convention also occurred at a time when "ethnic cleansing" in the former Yugoslavia and anti-refugee riots in Germany were reviving memories of wartime atrocities, slaughter, and mass murder.

Having survived the Soviets and the Nazis, my parents always had a keen smell for totalitarian rhetoric. My mother used to marvel at the ways in which some of Spiro Agnew's speeches reminded her of things that Stalin said. And she hated Nixon in 1960, well before I had any idea who this pasty-faced man was. "He's a fascist," she said with no apology for using the word. So I watched the Republicans in Houston in 1992 with my parents' eyes, with their history of murder, tragedy, and loss behind me as a warning.

I was angry. I was scared. I watched the faces, watched the eyes as much as I listened to the words. These were cold and angry men (and some women) who tried only briefly to hide behind Barbara Bush's grandmotherly persona. I call it a persona because she claims that George Bush is the "most decent" man she knows—a stunning assertion. But Mrs. Bush was just a diversion from the main business of the convention: hatred. It was pathetic after the convention when some Republicans totaled the number of speakers and said that Robertson and Buchanan were just two among them, and so not really important or representative. Prime time hatred cannot be diluted so easily.

The rhetoric of hate at the convention isn't new. Its bedrock is centuries of Jew-hatred, which is so deeply rooted in Western culture that it seems ineradicable. Jews have been demonized as Christ-killers, as murderers of children, poisoners of wells during the Black Plague, as religious and sexual seducers of good Christian men and women, as burrowing rats set on destroying capitalism *and* taking it over. We are eternal outsiders, eternal threats. "Germany Awake!" was one Nazi call to arms against this threat. Jew-hatred is the paradigm, and the charge of subversion, pollution, and disease has been a chief weapon used against us.

When Pat Robertson warned that feminism will force women to destroy capitalism, murder children, become lesbians, and practice witchcraft, that image of deadly and insane *conspiracy* draws on the deep reservoir of Western Jew-hatred and demonizing. Let's not forget that Buchanan admires Francisco Franco and Father Coughlin.

What was different was the vile new package that the Republicans were test-marketing: Superimposed on this Jew-hatred were racism, misogyny, homophobia, and xenophobia.

I never saw the people who tried to kill my parents. I only heard about them. Like the anti-Semitic Hungarian soldier in charge of my father's slave labor team who threw a hand grenade at him. The soldier missed, killing someone else, though my father still carries the burden of shrapnel and nightmares. Or the Polish woman who hissed at my mother as she was being led off to a concentration camp: "Good, now you'll get what you deserve!"

When I watched the convention, these were the faces I saw. I cannot listen to these men unquietly, without such memories haunting me.

And the Republican-controlled Congress elected in 1994 continues the legacy of intolerance. The Speaker of the House says that those who disagree with his plans aren't Americans. Dick Armey, the House majority leader, referred to openly gay Representative Barney Frank as Barney Fag. Armey blamed reporters for not keeping the story quiet, and then came up with ludicrous excuses for what he called a slip of the tongue. That was no mistake—it was a revelation of what he truly felt, and the sign that hate speech has found a home in Congress.

My parents were not paranoid in teaching me to pay attention to dangerous men. When Patrick Buchanan said, "Make no mistake, we are at war," he wasn't kidding. He *means* it. Watch his face next time he's on TV. Watch the faces of the Republicans now lording it in Congress. Look into their eyes. They could be your future.

Empty Memory? Gays in Holocaust Literature

13

Empty Memory? Gays in Holocaust Literature

There's a historical irony in the adoption of the pink triangle as one of the symbols of the gay and lesbian rights movement. We have actually known very little about what happened to gays and lesbians in the years 1933 to 1945. Our memory is in fact "empty memory," in the words of Klaus Muller, a gay consulting historian to Washington's Holocaust Memorial Museum. Muller uses that term because we are not "haunted by concrete memories of those who were forced to wear [pink triangles] in the camps."

In his introduction to the new edition of *The Men with the Pink Triangle*, a memoir by a gay Holocaust survivor, Muller notes that gays and lesbians have been among the "forgotten victims" of the Holocaust, rarely spoken of or studied. Likewise, homophobia has not been sufficiently examined "as an important part of Nazi propaganda, racism, and population politics."

Until this past year, Richard Plant's meticulously researched *The Pink Triangle* (1986) has been the major work in English helping to fill the historical gap (Frank Rector's 1981 *The Nazi Extermination of Homosexuals* is full of blatant inaccuracies). Plant's short study of Nazi persecution of homosexuals is valuable on many levels, not least for the clarity and strength of his writing.

Plant fled Nazi Germany for Switzerland in 1933, and later came to New York. His book opens with a moving prologue in which he describes both his fear at the time, as the son of a Jewish socialist, and the ways in which he and so many other Germans whom Hitler had declared enemies were unable to take Hitler seriously. One of Plant's friends was gay and was smuggled into Switzerland after brutal treatment in jail, but others were not so lucky. The book is thus in part fueled by a personal wish to bear witness to the suffering of his friends, though it never becomes polemical. Plant also clearly demonstrates the widespread taboo among noted historians and biographers on reporting gay experiences in the Holocaust.

Plant takes us from debates about the nature of homosexuality in nineteenth-century Germany through the Nazi persecution before the war and into the concentration camps. He starts the book with a crisp overview of German thinking (and lack of thinking) about homosexuality, and the ways this dialectic played out socially and politically. One of Plant's most distressing observations is that charges of homosexuality emerged in Germany as potent political weapons used by many different parties, not just the Nazis. Plant describes the German gay rights movement's repeated attempts to repeal Paragraph 175, Germany's main antigay law, focusing on a major figure in the battle, Magnus Hirschfeld. Hirschfeld was a walking composite of Nazi scapegoats: a liberal, Jewish, gay sexologist. His internationally renowned Institute for Sexual Research was one of the Nazis' early targets, and its ransacking, followed by a bonfire of its books and files, came a year before the well-known Ernest Roehm affair, or the "Night of the Long Knives."

It's easy to misread the killing of Roehm and his officers as mainly a brutal expression of Nazi antigay sentiment, but Plant disabuses us of that notion. In the summer of 1934, Hitler ordered the purge of the Brown Shirts (*Sturmabteilung,* or S.A.), the Nazi party's longtime private army. While its leader, Ernest Roehm, Hitler's friend and second in command, was openly gay, Plant says that his gayness was "a sideshow . . . never really the cause of his downfall." Homosexuality was used as a propaganda excuse to explain the purge—along with the far more serious (but bogus) charge of plotting against Hitler. The Nazis would likewise later use false charges of homosexuality in an attempt to weaken the Catholic Church, to eliminate youth groups that rivaled the Hitler Youth, and police the armed forces.

The Roehm purge served Hitler in a number of political ways. Roehm wanted his S.A. to absorb the German army, a goal that made its generals his bitter enemies. Hitler wanted the army to swear allegiance to him personally, rather than to the German state. A deal was struck and Hitler got his loyalty oaths in exchange for purging Roehm.

Murdering Roehm and eliminating the S.A. also eased party conflicts between paramilitary and political factions. And, according to Plant, the purge burnished Hitler's "image as a tough leader capable of imposing discipline and high moral standards on his own party." Far more insidiously, it established "the legalization of crime in the name of the state," setting a precedent for the murder of any German group conceived of as a state enemy, whether Jews, gays, Jehovah's Witnesses, or anyone else.

Plant devotes a bizarrely fascinating chapter to explicating S.S. leader Heinrich Himmler's background and the development of his "curious blend of cold political rationalism, German romanticism, and racial fanaticism." Plant admits that despite all the details, as with other Nazi officials, the biographical facts explain only so much; one is still left puzzled by the cold ferocity of hatred translated into murderous policies. Himmler's youth seems to have been filled with ongoing humiliation over his physical weaknesses and his family's low status and financial decline. Many adolescents harbor wild dreams of revenge against their perceived tormentors or as recompense for unbearable shame, but few get the power to enact them as Himmler did, in charge of the Final Solution. His inner

world eventually became a slumgullion of anti-Semitism, supersti-
tion, homophobia, paranoia about a Germany facing defeat by
a low birth rate, and lunatic fantasies for turning the S.S. into
Europe's new nobility, colonizing the continent with blond and
blue-eyed warriors.

Among the groups Himmler loathed, homosexuals were in his
view effeminate and pacifist criminals, with a dangerously conta-
gious disease to be found only in the degenerate bourgeois and
upper classes. This profile was not exactly sui generis: It was com-
posed of various views popularly held by a wide range of Germans.
Some of them sound a very contemporary note, calling to mind
current antigay rhetoric in the U.S.

Plant shows those policies being enacted into laws that are even
more cruel in effect than they are on paper because judges in Germany were increasingly given the latitude to punish any act at all
"if the inborn healthy instincts of the German people demand it."
In other words, they could completely overturn a basic principle of
Western law: Only acts that are officially listed as criminal can
be punished. Plant's chronology at the end of the book lists Nazi
legislation and activity against gays, Jews, and other targets year by
year. More powerfully than the narrative it is drawn from, this
schedule shows growing Nazi lawlessness masked as law.

Though gays could elude the Gestapo far more easily than Jews,
once they wound up in concentration camps, they fared very badly,
even though they were almost always among the numerically small-
est of the various groups of prisoners. All prisoners were supposed to
be brutalized, terrorized, and constantly reminded they were enemies of the state. But gays suffered in different ways. Homophobia
existed in the camps just as much as elsewhere. Attempting to join
an antifascist underground in the camps, you might be suspected of
only being after sex, or of spying because you might trade sex and
information to guards. Being classed as a state enemy didn't auto-
matically make other "enemies" feel any kind of bond, and gays

were "blamed" for sadomasochistic acts of guards or *kapos* (the prisoners appointed by camp officials to keep order).

Because they came from such widely divergent backgrounds, gays never united in the camps with any sense of group solidarity as did other groups. Few gays became *kapos* (who were mostly criminals or antifascists), and thus they couldn't intervene with camp officials or guards to help other gays. Unlike straight prisoners, gay prisoners also rarely received mail or packages from families or friends, who were ashamed of their incarceration, or afraid of being caught in the net of Nazi terror themselves. Finally, homophobic officials assigned gays to work details with the highest mortality rates, like quarries and cement factories. Some gays were also the victims of bizarre medical experiments attempting to alter their sexuality, and Plant estimates that as many as 15,000 gays died in the camps as a result of beatings, torture, starvation, or being worked to death.

Plant relays these horrors dispassionately, which is no easy achievement. But he warns that the persecution of homosexuals has a long history in Europe, and that the Nazi "hurricane of hatred" can be heard whistling in the rhetoric of fundamentalists calling for "holy war" against their society's "most vulnerable and vilified minorities."

It is likely that Plant's book is much less known than *Bent,* Martin Sherman's 1979 play about gays in the Holocaust. That is unfortunate. *Bent* is at times powerful art based on gay suffering in the Holocaust, but it's skewed in some not very obvious ways that create a distorted image of the Holocaust in general, and the role of gays in particular.

Bent is the story of Max, a shallow, coke-dealing, S&M-loving Berlin homosexual who winds up in Dachau after a 1934 roundup of homosexuals. In the course of two acts, he helps murder his roommate by finishing the beating an S.S. guard began, commits necrophilia to prove to the S.S. he's straight and thus deserves to wear a yellow star rather than the pink triangle (because it's supposedly "better"), has "verbal sex" with a fellow prisoner he comes to love, sees that man killed and kills himself—after donning the pink triangle.

Max is a frivolous charmer, impossible to care about, a man whose deepest insight into himself is that he's "a rotten person." If the play is an attempt to show that even men like him can learn to respect themselves and to love, it seems extremely cruel. Does it take Dachau to make someone deepen as a human being? If so much suffering is necessary, he must be hopelessly unfeeling—which he doesn't seem to be—so the play fails as the portrayal of a man's development into a *mensch*.

Before *Bent* opened on Broadway in 1979, New York papers were filled with articles about the play's success in London and interviews with the author. The common theme was the controversy the play had caused by asserting that Jews had it better off in concentration camps than homosexuals. Sherman was reported again and again to have done "years" of research in the British Museum, so the play was apparently based on accurate information. One negative American review said the only research one would need to write *Bent* was screenings of *Cabaret* and *The Night Porter*. I would add being tuned into urban gay life of the late seventies.

I saw the original Broadway production and have read the play several times since. I still think it's less the story of survival of human dignity under the most atrocious circumstances, or even of gay pride, than it is a sexual fantasy. The heavy sexual atmosphere is created in the opening scene with references to leather, chains, and cocaine, making the play feel at that point little more than a transposition of the late-seventies Greenwich Village to thirties Berlin. The atmosphere is heightened when Max's big blond pickup of the night before struts out of the bedroom nude.

In Dachau, Max's new friend Horst is openly gay and pressures Max to admit the truth about himself. Remember, he's not suggesting that Max come out to his parents at a family dinner, he's telling him to wear his pink triangle proudly in a concentration camp! It's grotesque. So is the fact that despite lifting and carrying rocks twelve hours a day, they manage to chat and flirt like they're at a bar:

HORST: Your body's beautiful.
MAX: I take care of it. I exercise.
HORST: What?
MAX: At night I do pushups and deep knee-bends in the barracks.

Horst doesn't believe it, but Max says he does it to stay strong, to survive. This ludicrous exchange is heightened onstage by the actors' undeniably healthy and attractive shirtless bodies, which nothing can disguise. And even when it was Richard Gere, his beauty could not blind me to the fact that his line was ridiculous. The play titillates the audience here by offering beefcake and saying, "Okay, pretend you're in a concentration camp and there's this really hot guy . . . !"

Max says that everyone in the camp talks about sex and misses it: "They go crazy missing it." This is nonsense. Richard Plant points out, as many other writers about the camps have done, that in a brutal and unpredictable atmosphere of terror, torture, starvation, filth, with no medical care, most people's sexual desires faded away. Prisoners were obsessed with *food*, not sex. While sex may have occurred, food was far more important and in memoir after memoir about the camps, you encounter tales of dreaming about food, fantasizing post-liberation feasts, or memories of prewar meals.

Given the play's sexual emphasis, it's not surprising that its real highlight is an act of fantasy sex achieved through talking. This act ostensibly proves that Max and Horst are still alive, still human. If anything proved that during the war, judging by Holocaust victims' stories, it was kindnesses like sharing food or helping the weak stand during a role call. Such acts challenged the barbarity of the camps and "salvaged the highest values" of Western civilization, in the words of Anna Pawelczynska, the Polish sociologist who was in Auschwitz and wrote *Values and Violence in Auschwitz* thirty years later. Max does perform such an act when he gets medicine for Horst's cold, but once again sex is central in Sherman's vision. To get the medicine, Max has to blow an S.S. captain.

Bent's greatest strength is shining a light on a much too unexplored region of the Holocaust, but it is often one-dimensional, poorly written, dramatically unconvincing, and even absurd. It is believable and historically accurate when a guard throws a prisoner's hat onto an electrified fence so that when forced to retrieve it, he'll electrocute himself. But that is undercut when a guard is unbelievably explicit and almost solicitous in his instructions to Max and Horst; he'd be more likely to shout some orders and beat the two men. The S.S. actually *knock on Max's door* for quite a while when they come to murder the man he picked up. The Nazis in this play can seem like figures out of a melodrama, but then the cardboard nature of the characters is well suited to a sexual fantasy. Over all, *Bent* reveals the limits of Sherman's imagination: He could not conceive of gays in a concentration camp without sex being central. Ironically, he confirms straight stereotypes about gay men, that even in that hellish environment, sex is still more important than anything else.

Just as distorting as *Bent*'s foregrounding of sex is the play's claim that Jews were more fortunate in the camps than homosexuals. This claim forces one to make obscene comparisons of suffering. Do we give points? How many for a man who has to beat his dying lover, as compared, say, to a woman watching a guard smash her baby against a wall? At various times Jews, Gypsies, and homosexuals were all subjected to insane medical experiments. Should we find some way to rank them? Wouldn't it have been enough to *add* the anguish of German homosexuals to the world's picture of the Holocaust—why must that suffering be greater? By letting a polemical aim distort his dramaturgy, Sherman in his own small way ends up aligned with those who for different reasons tend to ignore or blur the incontrovertible truth: Jews were always the Nazis' prime target of destruction.

Writing in the eighties, Richard Plant found assessing both the numbers of gay deaths and their circumstances difficult, given that some records had been destroyed, and many were unavailable behind the Iron Curtain. The situation has changed dramatically since the reunification of Germany, and we now have an invaluable book that can be read as a documentary companion to *The Pink Triangle:* the collection *Hidden Holocaust?*, edited and introduced by German historians Gunter Grau and Claudia Schoppman. This book is absolutely essential for understanding the Nazi reign of terror against homosexuals, as well as the radically inhuman mindset that can justify any means to achieve "moral renewal" and "moral stability of the state."

Grau and Schoppman have brought together and translated over one hundred important and representative items connected to Nazi persecution of homosexuals: Gestapo directives, speeches, legal discussions, letters, excerpts from books and articles, minutes of meetings, medical reports, newspaper articles. Amplifying Plant's work, their twin introductions create a clear framework for this mass of carefully annotated documents, many of which were in the former East Germany and unavailable to scholars before 1990. They are all deeply compelling.

The collection takes us from pre–Nazi era homophobia in Germany through the increasingly more punitive and bizarre stages of the Nazi campaign against homosexuality. Weimar Germany saw a burgeoning gay culture and an active movement to reform laws against gay men, as well as growing social and political homophobia. The early and mid-thirties brought bar closings, surveillance, beatings, censorship, and tougher antigay legislation.

From the mid-thirties on, the campaign escalated with stricter sentences, registration of homosexuals, "preventive detention" in concentration camps for some, and the institution of the death penalty for homosexual activity in the S.S. and the police.

While thousands of homosexuals were ultimately tortured, worked to death, castrated, and experimented on in concentration camps, Grau and Schoppman conclude that there was no *Holocaust* of gays—hence the question mark in the book's title. This assessment is based on the wide range of contemporary documents, including court records maintained with "Prussian meticulousness." Grau discounts the current wild estimates of as many as one and a half million gays killed by the Nazis, suggesting the figure is closer to 5,000, significantly lower than Plant's earlier estimate.

Grau finds that 50,000 gays were sentenced to prison during the period of 1933 to 1945, and 5,000 of those were deported to concentration camps. While serving a prison term could mean detention in a camp afterward, it wasn't automatic. The Nazis wanted to stifle homosexuality, but they had no interest in actually exterminating every homosexual. They wanted every man who could contribute to building the population to do so; they were obsessed with fighting anything they thought would result in "a general weakening of [the] nation's strength [and] military capacity."

How, then, are we to read the widely-quoted incendiary statements by Nazis like S.S. leader Himmler that consistently called for the "eradication" of homosexuals? After all, Himmler commended what he claimed was the ancient German way of dealing with homosexuals by drowning them in marshes. "This was not a punishment but simply the snuffing out of an abnormal life. It had to be removed, much as we pull up nettles, put them in a heap and set fire to them." Much of this rhetoric, Grau says, was propaganda meant for public consumption.

Grau holds that in this case we have unfortunately failed "to differentiate what was said in Nazi programmes from what was actually carried out." "Extermination" is thus an inappropriate term to describe the panoply of Nazi "decrees, directives, orders, and prohibitions" dealing with homosexuality.

In a framework of bizarre eugenics theory, what the Nazis really wanted to do was dissuade homosexuals from gay sexual practice through the use of intimidation and terror. If successful, these "punishments and deterrents" would supposedly keep the birth rate high, avoid contaminating public morality, and prevent the formation of antisocial cliques and the possible corruption of minors. The initial goal, according to Grau, was "reeducation through deterrence. And anyone who could not be deterred was sent to a concentration camp: reeducation through labor. Psychology was also brought into service: reeducation through psychotherapy." Gays were "watched, arrested, registered, prosecuted, and segregated . . . reeducated, castrated and—if this was unsuccessful—exterminated."

Despite these efforts, gays were never the subject of pogroms, and never faced the danger that Jews did in Germany or in occupied Europe, because *all* Jews were eventually targeted for *extermination*. Jews were doomed by their very *identity*—whether they practiced their religion or not. Gays could hide far more easily, and could avoid prosecution even if questioned by the Gestapo. Once arrested, if you maintained you weren't an active homosexual, you were freed unless there was proof to the contrary.

Grau makes clear that the Nazis did not have to create antigay policy and feeling in 1930s Germany. When they came to power, there was already "a police and judicial apparatus" in place, along with antigay law. Fervent antigay rhetoric also marked public debate. Though there were many calls for liberalization and tolerance before 1933, and there was an active gay rights movement, all this was balanced by the clamor for harsher laws, compulsory medical treatment, preventive detention, castration, and sterilization.

Under the Nazi regime, these demands were enacted into law so that ultimately, all homosexuals were victims, "whether they were interned in concentration camps, imprisoned by a court or spared actual persecution. . . . The racist Nazi system curtailed the life-opportunities of each and every homosexual."

If the fate of gay men in the Holocaust has been unclear, that of lesbians has been even murkier, as Claudia Schoppman writes in her separate introduction to *Hidden Holocaust?* Lesbians in the Nazi era were never uniformly seen as "a social and political danger capable of threatening the male-dominated 'national community.'" As the Nazis saw it, women could bear children no matter what their proclivities, and so lesbians were not threats according to "a majority of Nazi figures specializing in population policy." Debate continued for years about enlarging the chief antigay law, Section 175 of the penal code, to include lesbians, but it never happened, and thus lesbians were never prosecuted with any intensity. Some may have been interned as "anti-socials," but there's little evidence of their internment in concentration camps *as* lesbians.

What *is* certain, however, is that the Nazis wiped out a "collective lesbian lifestyle and identity" that had developed over several decades. Lesbians suffered "destruction of clubs and other organizations of the homosexual subculture, the banning of its papers and magazines, the closure or surveillance of the bars at which they met. This led to the dispersal of lesbian women and their withdrawal into private circles of friends. Many broke off all contacts for fear of discovery and even changed their place of residence."

All this took place in a climate of intense propaganda for motherhood, incentives for marriage, and the banning of abortion. From 1936 the Reich Office for the Combatting of Homosexuality and Abortion recorded all homosexual activity it came across, registered transvestites and abortionists, and monitored the production and sale of contraceptives and abortion-inducing drugs.

Hidden Holocaust? may be a collection of documents, but it is by no means dry. Throughout the book, voices leap out at us. Two of the most shocking pieces are in the earliest section. One is a published report of the Vatican's praise for Nazi efforts to ban obscenity. The other is a heart-wrenching anonymous appeal from gay soldiers to a bishop to intervene in the mistreatment and torture of gays held in prisons without being criminally charged. The desperate soldiers appealed not only to the love of Jesus but the Fuhrer's mercy—surely he would save them if he knew how they suffered. It's bitterly ironic to contrast this hope with an article from the S.S. newspaper declaring that homosexuals are out for a state controlled by other homosexuals, "just as a gangster wishes for a state run by gangsters." This, in a police state founded on terror.

Echoes of contemporary American intolerance make the book even more disturbing. There's an especially bizarre item that makes the current U.S. policy on gays in the military seem almost enlightened. It's a long series of instructions on suppressing homosexuality, written by the head medical officer of the German Air Force, that is so detailed it begins to read like soft core pornography. Medical officers are warned to see that men don't sunbathe or tell dirty jokes or wrestle or listen to sexy music because all of these activities (and many others) are bound to lead to an "overheated sexual atmosphere" and gay sex among "healthy, sexually needy young men" living "in close physical and psychological companionship."

It is important to have the solid understanding of the reality faced by gays in the Holocaust gained from Plant's study and Grau and Schoppmann's book before turning to the 1994 reissue of Heinz Heger's *The Men with the Pink Triangle* (first published in 1980), which appears with a new introduction. The account in Heger's book is the story of an anonymous Viennese gay man as told to Heger, but we now know that his name was Josef Kohout.

This crucial memoir offers rare insight into the period, but is also hampered in spots by everything Kohout could not have known about the larger context of his suffering. He mistakenly believed that gays were slated for the identical fate as Jews at the same time, that they died in the hundreds of thousands, and that sex between men was rife in every camp.

Kohout's memoir is one of the few by gay Holocaust victims because after the war, their behavior was still criminal in Germany. As many gay men were convicted in the 1950s and 1960s as during the Nazi era. Unlike other victims, their stories were not welcome, and the trauma of reliving what they had suffered was allied with their continuing, very real fear of exposure.

It is a harrowing story of sudden arrest, imprisonment and subsequent beatings, humiliation, slave labor, and torture. Especially powerful is the demonstration of how prisoners were turned into "dumb and indifferent slaves of the S.S." But although he was degraded and terrorized, Kohout was ultimately lucky. He survived six years of imprisonment because he was protected by kapos in return for sex, and because he eventually became a kapo himself and was spared a great deal of misery. Kohout was in no danger of starving, and could also get out of situations that might otherwise have led to his death.

Heger's book was originally subtitled "The True, Life-and-Death Story of Homosexual Prisoners in the Nazi Concentration Camps," but Alyson, the publisher, has unaccountably changed the subtitle to "The Life and Death Story of Gays in the Nazi Death Camps." It's a completely inaccurate and hyperbolic label. Kohout was a prisoner in concentration camps (Sachsenhausen and Flossenburg), not an internee with absolutely no hope of release in an extermination or death camp like Auschwitz or Treblinka.

We're not talking about a mere semantic confusion. Both types of camp "existed outside any legal restrictions," as Plant puts it. But however horrific the conditions he witnessed and endured, Kohout was not in an infernal factory whose purpose was the *destruction* of human beings. The introduction to the first edition of *The Men with the Pink Triangle*—not written by the same person as the second—made this important distinction very clear. It also noted that "at no time were homosexuals as such sent directly en masse to

Auschwitz," and that during the war there was a slackening of anti-gay persecution while the frenzied assault on Jews kept mounting.

For a sense of what the death camps were like, readers should consult a memoir like Primo Levi's *Survival in Auschwitz* or Terrence Des Pres's study *The Survivor*. The death camps were infinitely more brutal and inhuman than the camps described in Heger's book, and the events that took place there verge on the incomprehensible.

Pierre Seel's *I, Pierre Seel, Deported Homosexual*, is a very different memoir from *The Men with the Pink Triangle*, telling a story that is even less well known. Seel was interned in a camp for only six months. He also devotes a lot more time in his book to sketching his life before the camp — as a conflicted Catholic and fashionable young queer with chic clothes and hair — and to his postwar years of silence and torment.

An Alsatian, Seel at eighteen was imprisoned for six months in Schirmeck, an Alsatian detention camp (*Sicherungslager*) because he was gay. He was released for "good behavior," then drafted into the German army, where he served for four years until the war's end.

Homosexuality had not been illegal in Alsace, but before the war a policeman in Seel's town of Mulhouse bullied him into confessing he was gay. Seel had come in to complain about the theft of his watch, but he'd been robbed in a square known for gay cruising, which roused the officer's suspicions. Seel signed a confession and his name went on an illegally-kept list of homosexuals. When the Germans invaded France, Alsace was incorporated into Germany, and Mulhouse's police records became German property. German antihomosexual law demanded his arrest.

Seel was arrested, beaten, and tortured before being shipped to nearby Schirmeck. This camp imprisoned a wide range of Nazi enemies: "priests, prostitutes, Spanish republicans, deserters from the German army . . . black-marketeers . . . and British aviators captured in France." Gypsies and Jews, however, were transported east to the concentration camps and the death camps.

Trapped in Schirmeck until November 6, 1941, Seel was ground down by the "daily cycle of atrocities." Starved, beaten, and terrorized, he felt that "in the universe of inmates, [he] was a completely negligible element that could be sacrificed at any moment, indifferently, depending on the random demands of our jailers."

The most horrific moment came when he witnessed the murder of a former lover, Jo. While loudspeakers blared German classical music, Jo was stripped naked and had a tin pail shoved on his head. The S.S. sicced their ferocious dogs on him; the dogs ate him alive while helpless prisoners stood at attention.

It is a scene that Seel has never forgotten, but his nightmare wasn't over when he was released. His traumatized family was silent about his homosexuality, and the Nazis warned him that talking about the camp would bring reimprisonment.

Seel faced a new humiliation in the German army: "being forced to wear the swastika armband." In the next four years he survived "hand-to-hand combat in Croatia, bombs in Berlin and Greece, machine guns in Smolensk, and roundups by the Russians."

Pressured to marry after the war, he eventually did so because he felt he could not openly live a homosexual life. He was burdened by his past, his own silence, and fear of what people would say about his internment. He couldn't even be affectionate with his sons because he was afraid it might be misinterpreted. Seel gradually became an alcoholic and his marriage collapsed. Though he has come out in recent years to bear witness to the Nazi persecution of gays, and has fought with the French government for official recognition of his status as a "deportee," he is still—at seventy—angry and driven by the demons of his past.

Grau and Schoppman's book includes a document covering Seel's detention at Schirmeck: a letter from the German Security Police in Strasbourg that lists the deportees to Schirmeck as numbering 151. It is chilling to see Seel's individual story reduced to a statistic—but then, that's at the heart of Nazi barbarity. People were treated as things, and some, like Pierre Seel, have struggled for the rest of their lives to return from that hell.

Both of these memoirs are gripping and strange. Israeli novelist and survivor Aharon Appelfeld notes that such memoirs, written in "a search for relief," exhibit "haste, inarticulateness, and the lack of all introspection. It is as if what had happened had only happened outside them." This "literature of testimony" raises many questions about the human spirit, which its overwhelmed writers can barely approach answering. According to Appelfeld, we thus read the testimonies painfully aware that what is inside the authors "will never be revealed."

Robert C. Reinhart's novel *Walk the Night* is an earnest attempt to create fiction out of some of the material in *The Men with the Pink Triangle*, which he acknowledges as a source. Reinhart starts the book in 1970s New York, where a dying refugee German pianist, Leda Kohl, reveals the truth of her past to her son Peter. His father was actually a gay man swept up in the 1930s by the Nazis. She lost contact with him when she fled to America, and now wants to make sure he's all right. Peter sets off for Germany to find his father, who turns out to be a rich and successful designer. Though Peter decides not to reveal his identity, he does fall in love with Sybella, his translator-guide, and they get married.

The novel has a lovely scene in which Peter finds a record store in Germany whose window is full of his mother's recordings, and there's a chilling confrontation with antigay neo-Nazis in a small New England college at the novel's end. Otherwise, Reinhart's very ambitious book never really comes to life. The characters and the settings are unfortunately flat, and the novel shows its inspiration too clearly. There are long undigested quotes from books about the Nazis and gays, and the novel reads as if the idea—fiction based on *The Men with the Pink Triangle*—was never developed beyond early drafts.

I hope that *Hidden Holocaust?* is just the beginning of a new wave of eye-opening scholarship about the life and death of lesbians and gay men in our century's darkest years. I also hope it is read widely in the gay and lesbian community, where there is often deep ignorance of the Holocaust, and intolerance of Jews.

On gaynet, an electronic bulletin board on the Internet, and in many gay publications, I've encountered consistent misuse of Holocaust metaphors to describe any and all incidents of discrimination. The U.S. is often compared to Nazi Germany, and any public expression of antigay sentiment is likely to be dubbed "Nazi." Infringement of rights is routinely dubbed a first step on the road to a fascist state—"Look what happened in Germany," the argument inevitably seems to run. Republicans get called "*Ubermenschen*," and so on. If we lambaste Rush Limbaugh for his use of the insult "feminazis," how can we speak the same debased language ourselves?

It is offensive and pointless to use the Holocaust—a unique act of destruction—as a handy club to beat your opponent of choice, to score points in a debate. As Elie Wiesel has said, the Holocaust is not a metaphor of *anything*. To use it as such over and over is to completely misunderstand its reality.

I unsubscribed from gaynet last year after trying to make these arguments. I was attacked personally and as a Jew. I read grotesque accusations that the Jews were "trying to monopolize" the Holocaust, denying any special role to Jews in the Nazi slaughter. I was also accused of insensitivity and being ignorant about the "Holocaust against Gays." I got sick of explaining the Holocaust and the differing fate of Jews and gays in it to people who didn't seem to know much about either. As Robert Alter recently noted with disgust in *The New Republic,* "it is a little tiresome, at this late date of writing about the Holocaust," to have to note the obscenity of "the trivialization of the enormity of genocide."

ABOUT THE AUTHOR

Lev Raphael's collection *Dancing on Tisha B'Av* won a 1990 Lambda Literary Award. His short fiction has appeared in *Men on Men 2, American Identities: Contemporary Multicultural Voices, The Faber Book of Gay Short Fiction,* and many magazines. His essays have appeared in *Hometowns: Gay Men Write About Where They Belong, Living in the USA, Wrestling with the Angel: Faith and Religion in the Lives of Gay Men,* and other anthologies and journals. Raphael won the Crossing Boundaries Award from *International Quarterly* for a piece included in *Journeys & Arrivals.* He lives in Okemos, Michigan.